Y0-CCW-991

CENTRAL OFFICE
and
SITE-BASED MANAGEMENT

CENTRAL OFFICE
and SITE-BASED
MANAGEMENT
An Educator's Guide

Angela Maynard Sewall, Ed.D.

Professor of Educational Administration
University of Arkansas at Little Rock

TECHNOMIC
PUBLISHING CO., INC.
LANCASTER · BASEL

Central Office and Site-Based Management

aTECHNOMIC ᵖublication

Technomic Publishing Company, Inc.
851 New Holland Avenue, Box 3535
Lancaster, Pennsylvania 17604 U.S.A.

Main entry under title:
    Central Office and Site-Based Management: An Educator's Guide

A Technomic Publishing Company book
Bibliography: p.
Includes index p. 153

Library of Congress Catalog Card No. 98-85380
ISBN No. 1-56676-653-2

CONTENTS

Preface   xi

Acknowledgements   xiii

Chapter 1: Organization and Governance for School Districts   1

Constitutional Bases for School Districts 1
Governance: Structure and Role 2
State Structure and Funding. 2
Legal Status of the District. 3
Traditional Models of Governance 4
Recent Changes and Challenges 4
Stages of Educational Reform. 6
References. 7

Chapter 2: Superintendent: Manager, Leader and Facilitator   9

Superintendent and School Board. 9
Necessary Conditions for Working Relationships 10
Politics and the Relationship. 11
Superintendent as Manager 12
Superintendent as Leader 16
Importance of Style. 17
Superintendent as Facilitator 18
Superintendent as Communicator 19
Superintendent as Politician 20
Finding the Right Niche or Person 20
Conclusions 21
References 22

Chapter 3: Policy and Politics and Planning in the Central Office   23

Policy Defined 23
Policy Format and Focus 24
Policy and Planning 25
Policy and Site-Based Management 26
Law and Policy 27
The Importance of Policy Review 28
Policy and Reform 28
References 29

Chapter 4: Federal Money and Federal Programs in Daily Operations   31

Legal Compliance 31
Federal Programs Addressing Instruction 32
New Parameters 33
Importance of Understanding the Law 33
SBM and Chapter 1 34
Federal Programs Dealing with Disability 34
IDEA 35
Inclusion 36
ADA and Section 504 of the Rehabilitation Act of 1973 37
Federal Programs Relative to Student Welfare 38
Roles in Large and Small School Districts 39
Federal Funding for the Future 40
References 41

Chapter 5: The State and the School District   43

State Funding and Governance 44
Areas of State Impact on Schools 45
Pressures Faced by States 45
Central Office Response to Change 46
The More Things Change 47
Action Research 48
References 49

Chapter 6: Central Office Instructional Leadership: Curriculum Development and Supervision   51

Planning the Curriculum 53
Central Office Facilitation 54
Curricular Articulation 55

Testing and the Curriculum 56
Writing, Packaging, and Presenting the Curriculum. 56
Preparing Teachers for the Curriculum 57
Curriculum Supervision and Support 58
Curricular Maintenance and Modification 59
References 60

Chapter 7: Central Office Instructional Leadership: Personnel Development and Instructional Delivery Roles and Goals

61

Instructional Delivery 61
The Personnel Function 62
Collaboration and Team Building 63
Action Research 64
Personnel Development 65
Professional Development amid Restructuring 66
Instruction as Art and Science 67
Roles and Goals for Instructional Improvement 69
Legal Issues and Implications 70
References 72

Chapter 8: Special Programs for Special Needs

75

Special Education and Educators 75
Mainstreaming. 77
Professional Concerns. 78
Central Office and Inclusion 78
ADA and Section 504. 79
The Gifted Student 81
Compensatory Education 82
Vocational Education 83
Homeless and Migrant Students 84
Students with Health Care Issues. 85
*Students in Need of Disciplinary Intervention and
  Other "At Risk" Students* 86
Changes in Administrative Role 87
References 87

Chapter 9: Planning and Evaluation from a Central Office–School Partnership Perspective

89

From Vision to Plan 89
Planning Levels 90

Tools for Planning 91
Role of Central Office Administrators 92
Action Research 93
Evaluation/Assessment 93
Process Steps 95
References 96

Chapter 10: Central Office Business Functions 97

Linking for Efficiency 99
Technology for Curricular Efficiency. 100
Facilitated Curricular Development 101
Environmental Support. 102
Budgeting—District and Site 103
Centralized and Decentralized Activity. 104
References 105

Chapter 11: Public Relations, the Media and Selling the District 107

Public Relations Programs 108
Working with the Media. 109
Impact of Central Office Media Skills. 111
Passing a Millage: The Ultimate PR Test 112
Justification 113
Voter Encouragement 113
Caveats. 114
Additional Suggestions for Daily Public Relations Activities. . . . 114
References 115

Chapter 12: Legal Aspects of Central Administration 117

Constitutional Issues 117
Administration of Punishment 119
Search and Seizure 120
Rights of Speech, Expression, Press, and Religion 122
Finance and Desegregation 123
Daily Operations and Legal Questions 125
References 125

Chapter 13: The New Roles: Central Administration Redefined by Law and Practice 127

Restructuring the District. 127

Realigning Responsibilities. 129
New Positions/New Concerns 130
Unresolved Issues 132
Affirmative Action and Labor Relations 133
Desegregation Officers, Monitors, and Equity 133
The Decision to Restructure 134
Asking Reasonable Questions 135
References 136

Chapter 14: Community Perspective and
Central Office Functions   137

Productive Structural Change 138
Curricular Changes 140
Building Community Capacity 142
Methods for Engaging the Community 143
References 144

Chapter 15: Current Issues and Future Trends in Central
Office Administration   145

Models of Successful Change 145
Application to School Districts 147
Possible Scenarios from Restructuring 147
Requirements for Restructuring 150
Probable Scenarios If Change Does Not Occur. 151
References 152

Index   153

THE history of the superintendency and the development of the school board as the governing body within school districts parallels the industrialization and urbanization of the United States. As cities and communities grew, the number of schools and teachers working in those schools increased. As the number of schools increased, more principals were hired to oversee and assist the staff. Additionally, the use of custodians and other support staff became the norm.

More personnel and greater numbers of students in turn created increasing demands on the time and attention of the superintendent and school board. Following an industrial, or factory, model, the superintendent began to hire additional administrators to assist with the day-to-day operations of the schools and the school district. Over time and with the increasing complexity in educational operations, those administrators became (or were hired as) specialists in discrete areas of school operation such as curriculum, support services, personnel administration, and budget and finances.

Since the mid-1950s, with the advent of desegregation litigation, many districts have added staff to work specifically with court order compliance as well. Many large districts have added additional layers of administrators whose responsibility it is to work with schools and teachers. There are district curriculum area supervisors, supervisors of special education and gifted education, directors of student support services (guidance and social work), and even student hearing officers who address disciplinary policy implementation.

As bureaucracy has increased, schools have been controlled and monitored by an ever-increasing number of educational professionals. So complex has the organizational chart become in some school districts that the superintendent rarely visits a school and often has not more than an occasional passing contact with a principal. In a typical urban district with a student population of approximately 25,000, a superintendent was hired and remained in office only for one year. During that year, he visited no more than five of fifty schools. Given such a scenario, it is small wonder that some large-city superintendents, and indeed many superintendents of small and medium-sized districts, know little of what is actually going on in schools on a first-hand basis and that they may be reluctant to give up uniformity and control of schools' daily operations.

Even in some very small districts, with student populations of fewer than 1,000 students, there is tight control held by the superintendent either because principals and teachers are perceived not to be effective or because of pressure brought by the community and board to create uniformity in educational processes. (The fact that states have mandated curriculum has only heightened the tendency to consolidate power in the hands of a few individuals, thereby disallowing innovation and experimentation in schools and classrooms.)

Increasing public and governmental scrutiny of school districts and the passage of legislation such as IDEA, Section 504, ESEA, and the national goals were largely met with defensiveness and increased bureaucracy in the period of 1957 through the early 1990s. In recent years, however, there has been a call for innovation in education. Additionally, some sectors of the public are seeking a return to neighborhood schools coupled with the development of site-based management. The Home School and Charter School laws that have been passed in at least 50% of the states are evidence of public discomfort with the recent efforts of public education.

The tenor of this text is that site-based management is a necessary step in educational reform but that it can only be accurately defined and adequately achieved with a thorough reexamination of central office roles and responsibilities. It is not only time for central office administrators to become more visible in schools, it is also time for a collegial relationship and culture to be built within our nation's schools. That relationship must be predicated on a redefinition of roles and relationships as well as an increased accountability for everyone engaged in the educational process.

ACKNOWLEDGEMENTS

THIS book is dedicated to all with whom I have worked in education who have helped me gain an understanding of what must and can exist for the benefit of our students. My special thanks to my husband and parents and, in particular, to Angela Curry Maynard, who spurred me on in this enterprise and who critiqued my work. It is probably true that the best educators were blessed with parents who not only taught them and but also modeled good teaching.

CHAPTER 1

Organization and Governance for School Districts

Prior to any discussion of reform, an understanding of the educational process and its constitutional basis is necessary.

CONSTITUTIONAL BASES FOR SCHOOL DISTRICTS

BY virtue of the Tenth Amendment to the United States Constitution, school districts are the legally established frameworks for the governance and financing of public schools in the United States. That amendment, of course, reserves certain powers to the states. Among those powers is the right to establish and to regulate systems of education for the population of the several states. All states include within their state constitutions language relative to providing a thorough and efficient public education for the purpose of developing an educated citizenry. Such language specifically speaks to the state's interest in providing an educational system and to a consequent interest in requiring students to attend school within legally established age parameters.

School districts are constituted as a direct result of the state's interest in providing that education. School boards and superintendents are agents of the state as they labor to ensure educational opportunities for all students, measure student progress, address needs in relation to personnel and facilities, and promulgate policy. In fact, the roles of the school board and of the superintendent, as chief school officer within a district, are legally constituted within the statutes and regulations of the states.

1

GOVERNANCE: STRUCTURE AND ROLE

The structure of governance within school districts has evolved over time. That structure continues to change in this era of reform. Generally led by a policy-making elected board of directors and a salaried and certified licensed superintendent, the governmental entity called a school district has been in existence since the 1830s, when the first superintendents were hired in Buffalo, New York, and Louisville, Kentucky (Blumburg, 1985, p. 13). Although configured differently in different states and locales, the role and responsibility of the board, superintendent, and district employees in each state and locale are identical, that is, to provide a quality education, in compliance with state and federal law and local statutes, for all children resident within the district.

As noted, there are variable configurations and reporting responsibilities within districts. In some states, the board is appointed either by county officials or the mayor of the city when the district boundaries are contiguous with the city boundaries. In most situations, however, the board is elected by registered voters who are residents of the district. In some districts and states, such as Louisiana, members of the board are paid for their work. In other districts and states, board members are given office space at the administrative building. In still other districts, board members receive no compensation other than an occasional meal during evening board meetings and perhaps a reserved space in the district parking lot.

STATE STRUCTURE AND FUNDING

Most states have many school districts. In the state of Hawaii, however, there is one district that encompasses the entire state. Accordingly, although generally the funding base for school districts is some combination of state, federal, and local money, in Hawaii the funding base is federal and state money only. While many states configure school districts based on community boundaries, in some states, like West Virginia, Louisiana, Maryland, Florida, and Virginia, the "district" is contiguous not with the city but with the county. In Georgia, every county has its own school district, but there are more than twenty additional school districts specifically allowed in the state constitution. The extra districts are the continuation of certain districts that were already established at the time of the rewriting of that document. In states like Arkansas, there are even some districts that were created by special legislative acts, a practice that has led to court action when a specially created district subsumed part of an adjacent city as it grew into the county. The city had a school district of its own that was originally contiguous with city boundaries.

Throughout the United States, school districts grow, are consolidated and sometimes cease to exist as they attempt to meet mandated standards and a multitude of fiscal demands. The rulings in several desegregation cases have also impacted the configuration of school districts over time as districts have joined together in order to address the needs of minority students and to ensure a quality equitable education for all students. Such is the case in Atlanta, Georgia, where the DeKalb district joined with the Atlanta city schools in a desegregation effort and in North Carolina where the Charlotte–Mecklingberg District was created.

LEGAL STATUS OF THE DISTRICT

The school district, as a creature of the state, is bound by the laws and regulations of that state. State law generally is enacted by the legislature, which establishes the sources of funding for districts and parameters for the collection and use of funds within the district budget. Additionally, the elected school board and therefore the superintendent, who is hired by the school district board of directors or Trustees, as the case may be, become agents of the state. It is important to note that this is the case, for when issues of liability arise, immunity may be accorded to those officials when acting in their official capacities. (The issue of immunity will be discussed in some detail in a later chapter.)

State law impacts far more than funding, however. There are laws that regulate day-to-day business activities of the district, including the hiring and status of certified and noncertified (classified) employees. Law dictates the period of time during which the employees, generally certified employees, work without tenure, or "on probation." State law may dictate evaluation procedures and evaluation timelines for school district employees. At the very least, regulations that further define the law establish such guidelines. State law dictates due process procedures, in accordance with the United States Constitution and legal precedent, relative to the nonrenewal or termination of employees. State law also addresses issues related to other activities in which school districts are generally involved, such as purchasing and bid taking, debt management, the transportation of students, planning and construction of facilities, curriculum, and the parameters for student membership/enrollment in a district.

Under the auspices of state law, the school district, in most states, must answer not only to the state legislature and federal authorities, as appropriate, but also to a state education board, facilitated by the state school officer and appointed either by the legislature or the governor of the state. In cases in which the school district is desegregating and under court order, the board and superintendent must heed the mandates of the court, as embodied by the federal judge and the judiciary at the appeals level.

TRADITIONAL MODELS OF GOVERNANCE

Although the structure of the school district and its governing authorities have not changed in most states in recent years, the method of employing the powers given the board by the state and given the superintendent by the board has evolved during the past two decades and continues that evolution today. The traditional model for school district governance has been one in which the board is to make policy and the superintendent is responsible for the day-to-day management of the district. The superintendent as the executive turns to the board for action only in relation to the development of the district mission, the implementation of policy, the hiring and firing of staff on the recommendation of the superintendent, and the expulsion of students on the recommendation of the administration as represented by the superintendent. In other words, the role of the school board is found primarily in policy making and in its role as a judicial tribunal.

The superintendent is responsible for the disposition of that policy as it applies to district needs and operations. He or she must keep the board informed. Traditionally, most superintendents are not only the CEOs of their districts but also use their power and authority in a centralized manner. That is to say that most decisions are made at the central office level in regard to length of the school day, classroom composition, curriculum, staffing, allocation of resources, and expenditure of resources. While this approach has not been universal, it has certainly been the practice of the majority of superintendents in the United States.

RECENT CHANGES AND CHALLENGES

Since the publication of *A Nation at Risk* in 1983, however, school boards and superintendents have begun to change their approaches to, and their visions of, their roles and the roles of others in the school district. Under pressure from the press, the federal government, state legis-lature, and the public, some school board members have begun to delve into micromanagement of daily school district activities (i.e., adminis-trative responsibilities and prerogatives). The greater the pressure that comes to bear on the school district and on the individual board mem-bers, the higher the probability that school board members will evidence such behaviors in order to address public concerns and personal issues. It is important to remember at this point that board members who are elected have a constituency, and in districts in which that election is by zone or ward, the pressure on board members is even greater than when their election is at large. In the latter case, it is not voters who may not be personally known to the board member that bring pressure but rather it is friends and neighbors.

In such instances of board micromanagement, the superintendent must devote inordinate amounts of attention and time to the concerns voiced by the board. Truly, it is a primary role of the superintendent to work with and advise the board in addition to responsibilities to the district and its man-agement. However, when the board and its members engage in microman-agement, the attention of the superintendent is frequently diverted from his or her management and leadership tasks. Accordingly, school admin-istrators and staffs will begin to function independently of the central of-fice and district mandates. In many respects, this behavior was a hallmark of school and district activity during the 1980s.

Simultaneously, the federal government in the form of the U.S. De-partment of Education and also the National Governors Association ini-tiated a project in sixteen districts in eight states around the nation to fa-cilitate changes in educational governance, student achievement, faculty roles, and the principalship (Paulu, 1988). This project made no perma-nent national impact but did lead to other initiatives in administration subsequent to the Reagan Administration and to changes in standards and expectations in the various states. Currently, the schools of excel-lence program, the national standards relative to mathematics and social studies, and the National Goals are direct derivatives of these efforts.

Reform is in the air nationally. School boards and superintendents are finding that the tasks they must undertake are changing substantially. Property tax is no longer the base for funding in some states. Michigan, for example, voted to abolish the property tax as sole support base for the public schools and, in a popular referendum, substituted a mix of taxes, including property and sales taxes, and proceeds from a state lottery. In some states, too, the status of the board is being questioned. Site-based management has led to questions about the necessity for the existence of a school board for any purpose other than that of overseeing the management of finances. In fact, the city of Chicago has moved to a focus on school site management to the degree that the district is basically overseen by a financial board or a board of trustees headed by a respected business personality. Real decision-making power lies with the schools.

In several states, charter schools have been facilitated by the passage of state legislation that allows school staffs and their patrons to found schools separate and apart from the district. These charter schools operate outside of the mandates of school district policy and often with waivers from state and federal requirements relative to some programs such as Title I (formerly Chapter 1). Such changes, along with the increasing incidence of home schooling, have placed school districts all over the country in tenuous positions relative to their futures and to the continued financial assistance that are so necessary to their survival. Such changes have impacted and continue to impact the nature of the superintendency, the roles and responsibilities of the school board, and the functions of central office administrators in general.

STAGES OF EDUCATIONAL REFORM

In fact, one might argue, as did Bjork (1993), that there have been several stages of educational reform within the past twenty years that have deeply affected public education, including the roles of superintendent, board, and central office functionaries. The initial stage was that of national commission reports. These included *A Nation at Risk* (1983); *Making the Grade* (1983), which was the result of the work of the Twentieth Century Task Force on Federal Educational Policy; *High School* (1983), published by the Carnegie Foundation for the Advancement of Teaching; and *Action for Excellence* (1983), issued by the Task Force for Economic Growth. Stage one, 1982–1986, was at once reflective of and a response to the traditional central office role of top-down management, which tended to leave schools devoid of autonomy even within the instructional realm.

Stage two likewise reflected some national reports, such as the Holmes group study, *Tomorrow's Teachers* (1986), which caused significant change in many teacher preparation programs, and *A Nation Prepared* (1986); the work of the Economy Task Force on Teaching as a Profession. Bjork notes that in this stage some control began to shift from the district administrative level to that of the school. Paulu, previously cited, notes this in her writings about the sixteen schools that embarked on reform at the behest of the leadership of the National Governor's Association and under the aegis of then Secretary Bennett's Department of Education. Such a power shift in the domain of instructional leadership called upon superintendents, school board members, and central office personnel to enhance and utilize skills in collaboration, conflict resolution, leadership, and negotiation.

The final stage of change, according to Bjork (1993), began in 1988 and stresses a focus similar to that of the original one-room schoolhouse, the foundation of American public education, namely the child. Such a focus requires "new approaches in managing schools, working with empowered teachers, and providing instructional leadership" (p. 248) on the part of the superintendent. This is the stage in which school districts and their leadership find themselves throughout the country (Wallace, 1995). It is a stage in which, according to Donna Harrington-Lueker (1996), school boards are at bay (p. 18). Plans are in place in Chicago, New York, Washington, D.C., Cleveland, and several other large cities to change, if not abolish, the school board. Often, the proposed change is in the form of an appointed council or an institution that will have final authority in regard to schools and education. Although some of these proposed changes are political in nature, the major focus, according to Harrington-Lueker, is improvement in student achievement. Another focus is more directed, stable, and responsible governance for schools. It seems that the future of school boards and their governance in an era of reform is in the hands and actions of school board members themselves.

REFERENCES

Bjork, L.G. (1993). Effective schools-effective superintendents: The emerging instructional leadership role. *Journal of School Leadership.* 3:245–259.

Blumberg, A. (1985). *The school superintendency: Living with conflict.* NY: Columbia University Press.

Harrington-Lueker, D. (May, 1996). School boards at bay. *The American School Board Journal.* pp. 18–22.

Paulu, N. (1988). *Experiences in school improvement: The story of 16 American districts.* Washington, D.C.: OERI.

Power, K. (1992). "Visionary leadership and the waves of the future." *Updating School Board Policies.* 23(8):1–3.

Wallace, V. M. (1995). Superintendent: The instructional leader. Unpublished manuscript.

Webb, L. D., McCarthy, M. M. & Thomas, S. B. (1988). *Financing elementary and secondary education.* Columbus: Merrill Publishing Co.

CHAPTER 2

Superintendent: Manager, Leader and Facilitator

Consideration of the true roles and functions of the superintendent can lead to understanding of necessary conditions for effective leadership and management.

THE discussion of site-based management leads naturally to consideration of the real role of the school superintendent. The superintendent of a school district, be it large or small, is and must be a manager, leader, and facilitator. An examination of these roles will clarify traditional expectations and lead us to a discussion of the pivotal role of central office and its administrators, both line and staff, in the education of students.

SUPERINTENDENT AND SCHOOL BOARD

The superintendent serves a dual role relative to the school board, serving simultaneously as the board advisor and as an employee of the board. In the first role, the superintendent educates and informs the board, recommends policy and procedure to the board, mentors individual board members, acts as a resource for board members, and works the board to ensure unity and support for the district activities and strategies that the superintendent and staff develop as approaches to realizing the vision.

In the latter capacity, the superintendent must respond to the requests of the board, is employed by the board, is evaluated by the board, and depends on the board for contract renewal and salary increases. In point of fact, the superintendency is in an interesting yet somewhat unenviable position, namely that of being the primary advisor to the board while also being its direct employee. Additionally, the superintendent is generally not protected by teacher tenure laws but does operate on a multi-year renewable contract. The term "renewable" implies that he or she serves at the pleasure of the board and that in effect there is not tenure in the position.

The superintendent, when hired, is generally "brought on board" to serve or fulfill a specific agenda. It is not uncommon for a school board to seek a superintendent who will engage the school district in a desegregation suit or who has experience in "getting" a school district declared unitary. Some superintendents have particular expertise in such areas as dealing with the aftermath of teacher or other employee strikes, reorganizing staff, or reassigning or firing the upper-management echelon within a school district. Still others have curriculum reform as their forte. When a superintendent has completed the appointed task or failed to complete it to the satisfaction of the board, no matter what other changes or improvements have been brought to the schools within a district under the administration of that superintendent, generally he or she will either voluntarily move on or be forced to do so.

Paradoxically, there is no real appeal to the community as the board generally represents the community agenda. This is particularly true in situations in which board members are elected from precincts, wards, or specific geographical areas (i.e. not at large). It is safe to say that reform will not take place solely because a superintendent wishes to restructure schools or to implement site-based management within a school district. Rather, the board and/or community must be "sold on" or at least not resistant to whatever changes are proposed for implementation. As noted by Phil Schlecty, restructuring involves "changing the system of norms: the regular and patterned way of doing things" (Brandt, 1993, p. 8). The discomfort that accompanies change, absent at least tacit support from board and community, will generally place the superintendent in an untenable position as it relates to further employment or contract extension.

NECESSARY CONDITIONS FOR WORKING RELATIONSHIPS

This is to say that some superintendents learn the unpleasant consequences of their role when they try to manage their own "legitimizing agent" (Viteritti, 1983, p. 4), the school board, if that board is not accepting and ready to work with the superintendent and to hear his or her recommendations or plans. The key relationship among the superintendent, the board, and the community is predicated on politics. Since politics play a powerful role in the daily educational activities of the district, a successful superintendent must be mindful of them in all decisions and recommendations. This does not mean that all decisions should be political in nature but rather that the timing of decisions and recommendations will often be informed by political reality. Furthermore, the superintendent who is successful will always work the board as any good politician works a constituency to ensure understanding from the board members, to answer their questions and respond to concerns, and to garner their support, both individually and collectively. A successful superintendent talks to board members frequently, sometimes on a daily basis. He or she keeps the board informed about events in the school, particularly those of a negative nature, about which the board members may be contacted by patrons or the press, so that they will know how to respond, have the facts at their command, and, above all, not be taken by surprise.

POLITICS AND THE RELATIONSHIP

Since boards work within a larger political framework, the superintendent must also prepare the board for criticism that might follow educational decisions and arm board members with data and appropriate responses to such criticism. Many superintendents write memos to the board frequently. Of course, as in any other educational endeavor it is important to keep variant learning styles in mind. Written and oral communication address two modalities.

The idea has been expressed by more than one superintendent that in fact the relationship between superintendent and board is much like a marriage. The working relationship is a close partnership that needs time, attention, and deference. Communication and access between superintendent and board and with the public and its various constituencies are crucial. This political and public relations role in one that some superintendents relish and others abhor. Few superintendents, if any, are neutral to the political/public dimensions of the job.

Other roles a superintendent is called upon to play include that of the arbiter, negotiator, and often mediator within the district, among community interest groups, and between board members and factions on the board of education. "The superintendent plays the leading role in every decisional area about which board members [are] questioned" (Faber, 1973, p. vii). Additionally, the superintendent may need to act as a buffer between the board and teachers if the teachers happen to be unionized or to be members of an organization that negotiates with the district (as represented by a team, appointed by the superintendent, that develops personnel policy recommendations for board consideration). Frequently, members of the association will attempt to unilaterally lobby individual board members in hopes of gaining support for the teachers' position even prior to an administrative recommendation. It is up to the superintendent to keep both the board and the union in line by virtue of skill, knowledge, communication, and constant attention to detail.

SUPERINTENDENT AS MANAGER

The superintendent is called upon to oversee all functions and aspects of district operations. In small school districts, this implies that the superintendent may be personally in charge of finances, inventory, warehousing of supplies and equipment, maintenance of property and buildings, transportation, curriculum, staff development, and a host of other district business, student-related, and personnel tasks. In moderately sized districts, superintendents may actually have the support of assistant superintendents or directors of elementary and secondary schools. The existence of such positions filled by capable people allows the superintendent to devote more time to the board and community. Still, it is the responsibility of the superintendent to ensure that subordinates are knowledgeable and function effectively in their positions pursuant to their assigned tasks and responsibilities. The final accountability rests with the superintendent, and it is to this person the board will look should educational or support functions within the district go awry or should students fail to achieve as expected. In large, medium-sized, and small districts alike, more and more superintendents and, at their advice, boards are looking to private agencies and/or individuals to fulfill support roles within the district as needed.

While it may actually be financially smart for a large school district to keep an attorney on staff, it is neither necessary nor financially feasible for small school districts to do so. An attorney or CPA may be retained and used on an "on call" basis. Some districts have privatized custodial and transportation services. In Buffalo, New York, for example, each principal is allocated a sum of money from which custodial help is to be paid, and the principal then decides how to hire and whom to hire. Monies not needed may be used to support instruction; however, the principal, is held accountable by the superintendent for the expenditure of these allocated dollars and for the cleanliness and maintenance of the building and school campus.

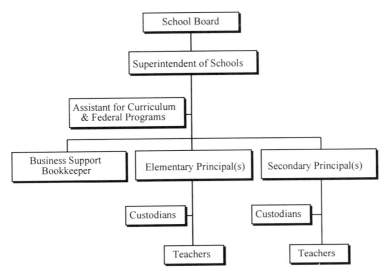

Figure 1. *Small District Organizational Model.*

While management issues may seem cut and dried, the most constantly visible component of the superintendent's work is that of district management. The area of management requires the broadest range of skills and expertise of all the tasks which a superintendent must undertake. It is true that management encompasses primarily a task orientation, but human relation skills are essential as well, for it is through the work and good offices of others that the superintendent manages the district. Figures 1, 2, and 3 attempt to show some of the ways in which superintendents have tried to share responsibilities within the school district organization in attempts to facilitate management and to increase available time for the superintendent to work with the board and to attend to community issues and other responsibilities.

Figure 1 depicts a small district in which the superintendent has elected to use the Assistant for Curriculum and Federal Programs as a staff position, thereby keeping himself or herself directly linked to and working with principals. There is no intermediate individual in a line position to whom the principals report or are accountable. It is not uncommon in districts with fewer than 2,000 students to find that there is an assistant superintendent in a line position who supervises the principals. Although such a person can be of assistance to the superintendent, flattening of the organizational chart can enhance morale, collegiality, and resource support for principals and teachers alike.

A superintendent who is committed to innovation and site-based empowerment of teachers and principals can facilitate such an outcome by personally meeting with principals and supporting principals' efforts while having the ability to assist or to hold principals accountable based on personal observation and involvement. Additionally, the staff curriculum assistance will be more welcome in classrooms and in principal-teacher supervisory conferences if he or she is in a support rather than an evaluative, role. Perceived safety with this individual will encourage teachers to try new methods in his or her presence and to discuss them openly in a self-critical and constructive manner.

Figure 2 depicts an organizational schemata in an intermediate-sized school district which for purposes of the text will be defined as having more than 2,000 and fewer than 10,000 students. In this case, the superintendent has structured the organization and the organizational chart by placing several line positions between himself or herself and the principals. It is generally the function of individuals in these line positions to take care of oversight of day-to-day school operations. The intended effect is to free the superintendent to work more closely with the school board. The usual effect is that the superintendent becomes increasingly isolated from what is occurring in the schools. He or she tends to become office-bound and to take the word of the intermediate level of management with regard to school operations and events.

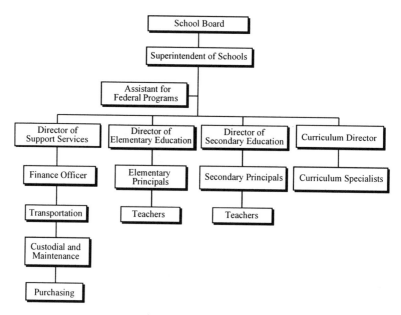

Figure 2. Intermediate-Sized District Organizational Chart.

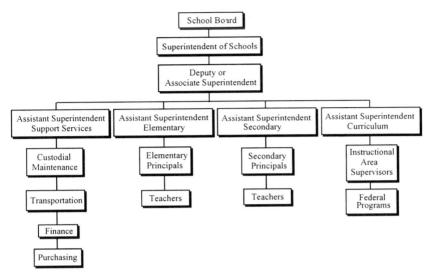

Figure 3. *Large District Organizational Model.*

In order to reorganize such a district, the superintendent should consider placing the curriculum direction and curriculum specialists in staff positions. The chart and district operational procedure should allow them to support the principals directly and to work in tandem with the elementary and secondary directors. Together the level director and curriculum supervisors should compose an administrative support team for the principal(s) at each instructional level, assisting with supervision, providing resource support, and helping to protect the institutional integrity of the school so that teachers can teach and the principal can be an instructional leader.

The principal should have direct entree to the superintendent, as should the other team members. Accountability would then be through the level director to the superintendent for evaluation purposes.

Figure 3 is a fairly typical depiction of the organizational chart and lines of authority in a school district that serves in excess of 10,000 students. On occasion, the position of deputy is called "associate." In fact, some districts feature associate superintendents for administration and for curriculum with directors of curricular areas reporting to the associate superintendent for curriculum, and assistant superintendents for elementary and secondary education reporting to the associate superintendent for daily operations or administration. This structure tends to be even more cumbersome than that which is depicted in Figure 3, for it divides authority over curriculum and authority over instruction and instructional personnel and creates opposing power bases, each of which works with teachers and within schools.

Even as it is presented in this text, the organization found in Figure 3 can be problematic as school districts attempt reform and move toward school site management. In the first place, placement of all curricular personnel in staff rather than line positions facilitates their ability to work effectively with teachers without threatening them because a staff role is that of a resource rather than an evaluator.

Second, if a superintendent is too burdened to address day-to-day contingencies and to work with the board, consideration might be given to a model that places a special assistant to the superintendent for daily operations on the organizational chart and deletes the position of deputy superintendent. Such as approach would flatten the chart, facilitating communication between the principals and the superintendent and between the assistant superintendents and the superintendent. It would also demonstrate the importance of the individual school and principal in a visual way by placing principals closer to the superintendent in line of authority and providing them direct appeal to the superintendent should any contentiousness arise between principals and their immediate supervisors.

The importance of flattening the organizational chart visually and in practice will become increasingly apparent throughout the remainder of this text.

SUPERINTENDENT AS LEADER

First, last, and always, the superintendent must be a leader. Leaders provide vision and direction. Leaders support followers and, in the case of a school superintendent, provide support to the school board and community in developing and seeking to realize the institutional mission. That mission is primarily instructional in nature. It is up to the superintendent to ensure that the focus of the entire district, from board to teacher to student, is on the students and their achievement. To ensure achievement, the superintendent must, by action and message, convey the necessity for excellent teaching, provision of instructional support in the allocation of resources, parental involvement, and the sacredness of instructional time. Wilson and Daviss (1996) make the point that "because teachers are rarely given enough time or support to master new techniques and materials, they often ignore them in favor of methods and materials they know well and feel that they use more effectively" (p. 127). The point is that continuous use of so-called "tried and true" methods and materials may or may not assist the teacher in providing effective instruction for students. As new research continues to address the need for diversity in instructional practice and the inclusion of technology in the classroom to enhance student learning and provide for learning differences among students, teachers must be free to try innovative methods and to vary traditional instructional practice. However, teachers must have the time and continuing education opportunities to enable them to learn and to appreciate the value and the efficacy of new techniques and theory bases.

Only the principal instructional leader can ensure that this will happen within a school. This leadership direction by the principal may only come when a superintendent assumes his rightful role as instructional leader within the school district to facilitate the work of innovative principals and to prod those who are not open to change.

IMPORTANCE OF STYLE

As leader, the superintendent must employ leadership style flexibility to ensure that followers will respond. Every leader has a dominant style, be it autocratic, laissez-faire, democratic, or benevolent. However, as noted by Hersey and Blanchard (1993), no one style is effective with all audiences or in all situations. Indeed, the autocratic leader may find himself or herself without a job if too much of that style is used with the school board or even with subordinates. Consequently, the leader must judge the maturity or readiness level of those with whom he or she works in order to ascertain the most effective way to approach communication and motivation in a given situation. With an individual, for example, a board member who is new and is therefore unable and perhaps unwilling to embark on a task for fear or failure or censure, the appropriate approach may indeed be autocratic, that is, to *tell* that board member what he or she should do or arrange for another more experienced board member to do so.

When working with an individual, for example a new principal, who is willing but not able to complete a task, the superintendent, no matter what his or her dominant style might be, should *participate* with the principal. Such participation is benevolent but also allows the superintendent to ensure understanding on the part of the principal. Often such participation implies not just discussion or response to questions but also encompasses the act of sitting down with the person and demonstrating how to complete a task. In other words, collaboration is effective and important until the new principal is comfortable with the task and understands policy or applicable procedures.

In the case of a parent or community member who is able to become involved in work with the school district or at a particular school but who feels unwilling to participate, *selling* is the appropriate approach.

This is a style which reflects the democratic leadership style of a superintendent. Obviously, the patron cannot be forced to participate. Selling engages the individual on his or her own level of ability and interest. Effective salesmanship is often necessary on the part of a superintendent as he or she shares his or her vision with an unwilling board or public concerning changes in policy, program, or even textbooks used in the schools. It is certainly a skill used within the context of millage elections in which superintendents and boards seek additional taxes for funding school district operating budgets, for retiring debts, or for capital outlay.

Finally, when an individual is able and willing to take on a task, the astute superintendent will employ a laissez-faire style. This style in no way represents a lack of interest but rather reflects trust and an acknowledgment of the skill of the other in performing the task, whatever it is, as it relates to realizing the goal of providing quality education for students and fulfilling the district educational mission. Such a demonstration of trust empowers others to act and to assume leadership roles themselves.

Leadership implies the building of a team. Leadership may seem to be evidenced primarily by human relations skills but, in fact, as demonstrated by theorists such as Ouchi, both task and human relations skills are essential to good leadership. In order to work effectively with the team and to ensure that team members include central office staff and school site staff, the superintendent is called upon to share not only the vision but also to demonstate a visible commitment to reaching it. To that end a superintendent must understand essential tasks, be able to explain them to others, and be able to perform them with some degree of expertise. In other words, as a leader, the superintendent must be a generalist as well as a specialist in both the role of leader and the role of manager.

SUPERINTENDENT AS FACILITATOR

Facilitation is the name of the game for a successful superintendent. It is the superintendent who "makes" change occur. The superintendent builds the culture of the district just as the principal helps build the culture in a school. In recent years, however, superintendents have averaged a tenure of fewer than three years nationally (Crowson, 1987). This is hardly time to facilitate any changes. Certainly it is not sufficient time for culture building. If we define culture as the way we do things in the district, three years or less is not ample time for tradition building or for the development of rituals. It is hardly time to identify heroes and create the mythology is a hallmark of culture.

It is the superintendent who ensures that all is in place for smooth board meetings (e.g., the agenda, appropriate preparatory materials, and background information). It is the superintendent who marshalls and guides the assistance provided by central office staff in preparation of reports, press releases, and research. It is the superintendent who provides support to the board members, listens to their questions, and facilitates resolution of interboard disputes. It is the superintendent who protects the board members and who guards the integrity of the staff.

It is primarily the superintendent who facilitates change in the public mind through press releases and presentations to civic clubs and PTAs, and by means of his or her behavior in the public eye. It is the superintendent who prepares public, board, faculty, and staff for disappointments and who ensures that their successes are appropriately celebrated via recognition at board meetings, congratulatory notes, and public recognition in venues other than the school. Without these conscious efforts by the superintendent, good morale, the change process, and ongoing success for students and schools will not be facts of district life.

SUPERINTENDENT AS COMMUNICATOR

The superintendent is his or her own best PR agent. Among the roles that every superintendent must play is that of dealing effectively and positively with the media. It is true that bad news sells better than good news. Still, there are methods for blunting the potential damage of bad news to the school district and individual staff members if the superintendent is proactive in sharing information and solutions to difficulties with the press. Successful superintendents realize that TV sound bites are very short. Consequently, they ensure that what they say to the visual media is concise and to the point. Successful superintendents realize that stories in the print media may contain all of the facts but that members of the public are likely only to read the opening few paragraphs of a story. Consequently, they ensure that any press releases coming from the district place all pertinent information in the initial paragraph. Successful superintendents have identified competent individuals who can communicate well and strategically placed them to respond to the press and to notify the press of positive stories and photo opportunities.

Successful superintendents keep their staff and the board updated. They do not hoard information but rather share it as needed with those parties who are responsibile for the successful functioning of schools and programs within the district. Successful superintendents generally have regular cabinet meetings with central office staff and at least one principal representative to keep current with ideas, concerns, and issues and to discuss and brainstorm solutions to problems and plans for the schools and the district itself. Successful superintendents understand that communication is key to team building and that communication is a two-way process. They know that communication involves listening, the thoughtful decoding of information, and the ability to ask strategic questions.

Finally, superintendents who are effective communicators realize that they themselves do not have all of the answers. Therefore, the public as well as school principals and faculty are engaged in dialogue with them and with central office administrators. Such superintendents ensure that opportunities are created and provided for such discussion and that responses to the discussion and ideas of others are given.

SUPERINTENDENT AS POLITICIAN

It is easy to understand from the discussion so far that the job of the superintendent is highly political. It is a job that is perhaps more tenuous than that of any politician. The superintendent may be terminated at any time at the will of a board that responds to the public. Even if a contract is bought out by the board, that is tantamount to a termination.

Every decision made by a superintendent and each recommendation to the board impacts some constituency within the district. Those constituencies are not limited to students, faculty, and parents but also include ministers, civic groups, real estate firms, and private businesses, among others. The factors with which a superintendent deals each day are perhaps the most important in the lives of those in any one of the multiple constituencies, namely, their money, their children, and their own memories of what a school should be.

FINDING THE RIGHT NICHE OR PERSON

The search for a superintendency and the search by the board for a superintendent are daunting tasks. Decisions must be made by the board relative to the qualifications of the individual who is sought. Beyond that, the board must decide whether it wishes to conduct the search itself or to hire consultants to do so. Additionally, there is an important trade-off about which the board must make a decision, namely, whether to hire someone who knows and has worked in the district and who, by virtue of that knowledge, is a known quantity or to hire someone who is unknown to the district and its constituents and therefore knows little about the district.

There are pros and cons for each approach. Someone who is known may have made decisions that angered or alienated some people in the district in the past. The known applicant may even come to the superintendency with a split board based on some of those past decisions. On the other hand, that individual is ready to begin work without taking time to learn about the district and its staff, its strengths, and its needs.

Each individual who aspires to a superintendency must make a similar choice, that is, whether to apply for a superintendency in the district in which he or she is known or to seek a superintendency outside of the district, region, or state of current employment. Whatever choice is made for whatever reasons, those who are school superintendents face formidable tasks from the first day of their employment as they seek to lead, manage, and facilitate change and progress for the students and community with the team they inherit and build or rebuild at the central office.

CONCLUSIONS

The short tenure of many superintendents in the United States lends credence to the importance of the role as politician. It also lends strong support to the importance of good management and leadership skills on the part of a school district CEO. In the midst of change and calls for reform, controversy will often swirl around the superintendent and the board.

Superintendents who fail to evidence good fiscal skills or who fail "to deliver higher test scores fast enough . . . find themselves discredited" (Johnson, 1996, p. 60). Consequently, if superintendents are to have the time (tenure) to ensure that change takes place in a school district, it is imperative that they empower, encourage, and support the efforts of principals and teachers in making change. According to Johnson, this demands good ongoing communication, collaboration, and support for the efforts of others without taking personal credit. In a sense, the key reform role of a superintendent is that of coach—one who has and shares the vision, draws up the game plan, and sends the players out to fulfill their roles, all the while providing support and encouragement with occasional correction.

REFERENCES

Brandt, R. (1993). On restructuring roles and relationships: A conversation with Phil Schlechty. *Educational Leadership,* 51(2): 8–11.

Crowson, R.L. (1987). The local school superintendency: A puzzling administrative role. *Educational Administration Quarterly,* 23(3): 49–69.

Faber, C.F. (ed.) (1973). *School board conflict, cohesion and professional negotiations.* Lexington, KY: University of Kentucky.

Hersey, P. & Blanchard, K.H. (1993). *Management of organizational behavior.* Englewood Cliffs, NJ: Prentice Hall.

Johnson, S.M. (March 13, 1996). Turnover in the superintendency: A hazard to leadership and reform, *Education Week.* pp. 47, 60.

Viteritti, J.P. (1983). *Across the river: Politics and education in the city.* New York: Holmes and Meier.

Wilson, K.G. & Daviss, B. (1996). *Redesigning education.* NY: Henry Holt & Company.

CHAPTER 3

Policy and Politics and Planning in the Central Office

As in any successful enterprise, strategic planning is crucial to the success of school district educational enterprises.

CENTRAL office administrators have a key function in the development of policy for the school district. If asked about policy, many individuals would doubtless indicate their belief that it is fairly benign and rarely inspires great controversy. Those individuals would be wrong. Policy has the impact and effect of law in a school district. It can only be made by the school board, though it is recommended by the superintendent with advice from his staff. Policy must reflect the intent and parameters of state and federal statutes, and it dictates much of what schools, personnel, and school districts may and may not do. "A policy is a general statement of objectives that guide organizational action" (Hoy & Miskel, 1996, p. 270).

POLICY DEFINED

According to Furst (1992), the common elements of policy are that policy:
- is a formal act
- has an agreed-upon intent
- is sanctioned or approved by an institutional body or authority
- provides a consistent standard for measuring performance

"Through its policies, a board of education provides direction for the school district while allowing administrative discretion in their implementation" (Clemmer, 1991, p. 11). This is the ideal, but if board mem-

bers come to their positions with their own agendas and the desire to pro-
mote only those agendas, then the policy-making role becomes
somewhat muddled, for, as previously noted, those same board members
may become embroiled in management. This interaction is but one of the
many facets of politics in policy.

Powers (1996), in an article in *The School Administrator,* notes that
when board members lose sight of their role, the issues that come to the
school board are "not issues of policy" (p. 52). He further notes that
"the continuation of such faulty governance procedures eventually
could be tragic to a democratic society by discouraging good school
committee members, superintendents, and school staff, and hurting
educational systems" (p. 52). The making of policy is a pivotal role for
the board. Policy made by the board determines the direction of the district and, in large part, the legality of actions and activities within the
school district.

POLICY FORMAT AND FOCUS

Of course, the board must rely on the expertise and knowledge of the
superintendent as a basis for consideration of recommended policy
changes and/or development. The superintendent, in turn, can rely on
the published materials relative to policy that can be obtained from the
National School Board Association. There is, of course, a nationally
shared format for policy. For example, items coded A relate to the
foundations and basic commitment of the school district, including legal status, mission statements, and evaluation of staff and programs.
Items coded B relate to school board governance and operations. Items
coded C address general school administration. Other codes relate to
fiscal management (D), support services (E), personnel (G), negotiations (H), instruction (I), students (J), and additional topics such as
school-community relations. Each section has several subsections. For
example, within the section on negotiations (H), subcodes include
board-staff relations (HD) and recognition of staff to meet and confer
organizations (HGA). Those sections dealing with personnel, instruction, students, and support staff contain the greatest number of subsections. The format for each section, suggested codes for subsections,
and suggested language for the wording of individual policies are all
included in the National School Board Association policy book.

As policy is made, regulations are written for board, staff, and community awareness and/or for board adoption according to practice in the

individual district. Staff research should and generally will ascertain those laws (state statutes) that relate to the policy and annotate them in conjunction with the policy. For example, a policy that relates to the non-renewal of certified personnel would be accompanied by a citation to state law relative to teacher fair dismissal. (Teacher fair dismissal will include references to due process, an explanation of liberty and property interests relative to the position held, and state tenure law if such exists.) A policy on vandalism would include a citation to state law relative to legal penalties for such activity. Two relatively new areas in which school districts have written policy are sexual harassment and AIDS, which may be included with the latter policy generally listed within the policy on infectious/communicable diseases.

POLICY AND PLANNING

Policy is a major factor in strategic planning. Good policy must be in place before a school district can write regulations or develop procedures for governance, compliance with the law, and the addressing of incidents that might arise in day-to-day operations. In this period of reform, policy provides the basis for and parameters of site-based management and the related planning. Policy allows the district, as represented by the superintendent, board, principals, faculty, and staff, to address the mega-, macro- and micro-communities with which all personnel are engaged on a daily basis. Kaufman (1992) defined these as those strategic groups whose needs must be met, if not in the present then in the future, by virtue of educational planning and activities that take place within the district and its schools. The mega level generally denotes the ideal vision for societal outcomes (Kaufman, 1992, p. 30), while the macro and micro levels of planning relate to organizational and individual or small-group issues respectively (p. 16). Each of these levels and the associated concerns must be aligned within the planning process. This planning process is enfolded in and itself parallels the relationship among policy, regulations, and operational procedures.

Policy, of its very nature, addresses the broad view, the mega level of concern. Policy has a practical orientation and provides guidance for actions taken and decisions made within a school and within the district (Gallagher, 1992, p. 4). Duke and Canady (1991) define policy as "any official action taken at the district or school level for the purpose of encouraging or requiring consistency and regularity" (p. 2). Policy includes and formalizes district goals, which by the nature of the school board and school governance in the majority of school districts in the United States are largely reflective of community goals and objectives. Occasionally, policies that one district might have on a specific topic, for example, nepotism, are not found in the body of policy in another district. Such differences generally reflect the fact that nepotism (or whatever the issue might be) has not been a problem in need of address within that district. In this period of change, however, greater similarity in policy seems to be finding its way into the manuals of large and small, urban and rural, special and comprehensive school districts across the country.

POLICY AND SITE-BASED MANAGEMENT

The public, legislators, and educators are calling for more site-based management, individual teacher authority and autonomy, and even for the opportunity to charter their own schools or to resort to home schooling. In response, school districts, as represented by boards and superintendents, are reviewing and adopting policy models which have proven successful in addressing these issues in other venues. The public in many sections of the country has become increasingly involved in the selection of materials for instructional purposes and in the range and types of literature and media that are available to students within school libraries. In the face of such involvement by both liberal and conservative patrons of schools, school boards have found it necessary and prudent to adopt policy which speaks to not only the educational intent and goals for instruction within the district but also to the process for considering complaints relative to materials adopted for educational use and procedures for review of materials.

Policy clearly relates not only to instruction but also to curriculum. The role of policy implementation has been impacted during the current era of reform, however. No longer do effective school boards and superintendents reserve the implementation of policy to themselves. As noted in Chapter 2, the era of the authoritarian, hierarchical organization is, if not gone, definitely on the wane. The current trend, in line with school site management or site-based management (SBM), is for policy with regard to management of resources (i.e., budgeting), to be made at the site closest to the expenditure and line item need. The allocation of such resources is generally still reserved to the central administration and reviewed by the board during the annual budget presentation and subsequent financial reporting.

Similarly, although the policy of most school districts directs that central office administrators must be engaged in the process of seeking, investigating, and conducting preliminary screenings relative to candidates for employment within the school district, current practice generally dictates that the actual interviewing and recommendation for hiring emanate from the site at which the individual will be employed. Evaluation of site personnel also falls within the bailiwick of the site administrator, sometimes with the assistance of central office administrators. (Of course, the evaluation of the site administrator, be that administrator certified or noncertified, still is the responsibility of the assigned central office administrator or of the superintendent himself or herself.) Both formative and summative evaluation are responsibilities of central office and site administrators.

LAW AND POLICY

Policy that comports with the law, both federal and state, is the vehicle by which externally mandated programs are inculcated into the district. Chapter or Title 1 [as it has variously been styled since the federal ESEA program (1965)], special education programs (IDEA), and the Americans with Disabilities Act (ADA), as well as Act 504, are all implemented within the schools and other district workplaces, as appropriate, and managed by central administration and site administrators alike. Translation and application of federal titles such as Title IX and Title VI to activities and individuals also is the responsibility of the central administration and must be reflected in policy.

"When examining the full range of leadership functions associated with any organization, certain processes fall logically into the domain of the broadest most centralized units, whereas others fit better into the directly operational level" (Sage & Burrello, 1994, p. 147). Clearly, policy development is a major responsibility that is within the domain of the central administration as visibly respresented by the superintendent and board. In fact, policy is a key to the actualization of the vision of the board and superintendent and the mission of the individual school district.

Policy review is an ongoing crucial component of the process. Such review will take place naturally when there are issues of concerns raised as to the appropriateness or timeliness of existing policy or the absence of needed policy. It is, however, the responsibility of the central administrative staff to keep the superintendent apprised of changes in the law or best practice which will mandate policy changes. Policy is the vehicle through which norms of conduct are established for both employees and students within the district. Inherent in policy are frameworks for decision making and daily district operations. Consequently, policy must be reviewed, questioned, analyzed, modified, and adopted on a regular basis. Since administrators are legally bound to act within the framework of policy, failure to update policy appropriately may hamstring the work of the administrator, the teachers, and consequently, the entire school district.

THE IMPORTANCE OF POLICY REVIEW

Designated central office administrators must consistently and constantly review policy to ensure its continued compliance with law and applicability to practices, students, and employees within the district. Such efforts keep the board, administration, and schools in compliance with the law and operating with the best interests of the mega-, macro- and micro-constituencies in mind. Through such efforts the board, administration, and schools maintain a forward-looking and forward-thinking posture relative to academics, extracurricular activities, students, personnel, and support services, as well as virtually all district engagements and areas of concern or focus. Calculations of the risk in adopting innovative policy in the face of potential legislative changes but in a community that does not welcome change is also a vital component of policy review and administrative practice.

According to Gallagher (1992), the key issues a district must address in consideration of policy adoption or change include:

- technical feasibility
- effectiveness
- economic feasibility
- goals
- objectives
- administrative operability

POLICY AND REFORM

Each district will view these criteria in different ways. They are constants that must factor into decision making, however. The era in which policy could be overly broad or vague is over. The thoroughness with which the state, the board, the employees, and the constituencies of school districts scrutinize school goals, functions, and administration make clear, effective policy and a thorough process for its review and adoption "musts" in an era of education questions and reform.

REFERENCES

Clemmer, E. F. (1991). *The school policy handbook.* Boston: Allyn & Bacon.

Duke, D. L. & Canady, R. L. (1991). *School policy.* NY: McGraw-Hill.

Furst, K. S. (1992). *Shaping school policy.* Newbury Park, CA: Corwin Press.

Gallagher, K. S. (1992). *Shaping school policy.* Newbury Park, CA: Corwin Press.

Hoy, W. K. & Miskel, C. G. (1996). *Educational administration: Theory, research and practice.* (5th ed.) NY: McGraw-Hill.

Kaufman, R. (1992). *Mapping educational success.* Newbury Park, CA: Corwin Press.

Powers, W. M. (1996). Today's superintendents: Imperiled or just challenged by board behavior? *The school administrator,* 5(53): 51–53.

Sage, D. D. & Burrello, L. C. (1994). *Leadership in eduational reform.* Baltimore: Paul H. Brookes Publishing Co.

CHAPTER 4

Federal Money and Federal Programs in Daily Operations

Although federal dollars do not comprise a large percentage of a district budget, federal regulations have a major impact on operations.

FEDERAL programs have been important components of public school operations and some private school operations since before the beginning of the so-called "baby boom," which officially began in July 1946. Among those programs which have ongoing impact on all students are the federal lunch and breakfast programs, the sale of food commodities to schools, ESEA, the Title or Chapter programs, IDEA (Individuals with Disabilities Education Act, a correlate of P.L. 94-142), Title VII, Title IX, ADA, Americans with Disabilities Act, and the related Section 504 of the Rehabilitation Act of 1973.

LEGAL COMPLIANCE

The role of central administration, no matter what its configuration, is to ensure legal compliance with the terms and requirements of federal legislation as it impacts and relates to schools. Generally grant applications are generated at the central office level and are managed there in terms of assurance of correct expenditures, filing of appropriate reports, and fulfillment of requirements attendant on the paying of salaries based on soft (grant) money such as SSI and FICA. These roles alleviate somewhat the work of the school-based administrator even in the most site-based school districts. (What will happen with regard to grant money in the context of charter schools is an issue yet to be resolved, as charter schools are by their very nature separate and distinct from the school district during the life of the charter.)

In cases in which the grant application and basic management emanates from the school, the central administration generally assists with grant preparation. The superintendent presents the grant for board consideration and approval prior to the submission of the application. Of course reasons for this process include accountability, protection for the district, and communication with the board and public concerning district activities as approval takes place within the context of a public board meeting.

FEDERAL PROGRAMS ADDRESSING INSTRUCTION

In 1957, Sputnik was projected into space by the Russians. That event, more than any other, began to raise questions in the minds of many Americans concerning the worth of a public school education. The immediate federal response was to initiate programs to provide funding designed to improve instructional practice and student learning outcomes in mathematics and science. As we now know, funding in and of itself does not impact practice. It does provide additional money to be spent for instructional aides within the classroom. Therefore, within approximately seven years, under the aegis of the Johnson administration, Congress began the process of appropriation of instructional support and funding for specified uses predicated on strict regulations and procedures.

The first major effort within this funding practice strand was ESEA, the Elementary and Secondary Education Act of 1965. From this act emanated Chapter (Title) 1 and 2 programs. As most educators are aware, these funds, set aside by congressional appropriation, are allocated to school districts based on the number of low-SES (socioeconomic status) students who attend schools within the district and also on remediation needs within the district. The district in its application process submits plans for expenditure of the funds it would receive for the purpose of remediation of students in the lowest quartile on standardized tests in the areas of mathematics and language arts.

There are and have been significant limitations on the expenditure of Chapter/Title funds, however. (Please note that the designation "Chapter/Title" relates to the fact that during the life of this act, the name of the program has varied.) The limitations are that Chapter/Title 1 moneys may be used only for those identified students in need of remediation, and no student who participates in or benefits from other federal programs, such as special education students, may participate in Chapter/Title 1 programs or benefit from that funding. Chapter/Title 2 money is designated for the purchase of instructional media materials, in other words, library materials.

NEW PARAMETERS

Recently, the chapter programs have been changed. Under the latest rendition of the law and its attendant regulations, which took effect July 1, 1995, more money is granted to high-poverty schools and less money to those schools with a lower percentage of low-SES students, no matter what the remedial needs of the school population might be. In fact, under the new regulations, many high-poverty schools which have high-achieving students are receiving more funding for remediation than they did in the past.

Additionally, fewer nonpublic schools are being granted access to remedial services for their students under what is currently styled Title 1. In times past, private and parochial schools with high percentages of low-SES students could access such services for students in need of remediation. Although these schools did not receive direct funding due to the need for the state to remain neutral in matters of church and state relationships, public school teachers, materials, and sometimes buildings were used for the private and parochial students benefiting from the students with remedial services.

Efforts are also being made to tie the Chapter/Title 1 programs to the achievement of the national standards as they are being established (Miller, 1995, p. 27). Additionally, money may now be used on a school-wide basis and combined with other federal funds to ensure student learning. An important role for central administration, especially in light of these and other reforms, is identifiable at this juncture.

IMPORTANCE OF UNDERSTANDING THE LAW

If site administrators have not read the new law and are not conversant with it, then the role of central administrators under the leadership of the superintendent is to ensure full understanding of the law and its new parameters for all educators, particularly those who are used to operating under the "traditional" requirements, and to ensure compliance with the law. In fact, it is true that most school site administrators have no time to read the voluminous regulations that accompany changes in the law. The daily tasks of school administration virtually preclude careful tracking of variations in regulations and processes. Consequently, in order for schools and school districts to maintain a strong positive relationship with federal agencies and regulators and to protect and maintain grant money being received, the role of central office administrators who work with federal programs and grantsmanship is crucial. This is true within both small and large school districts.

Finally, as is the case with any grant received by a school or district, yearly reports of progress and accounting of expenditures is a component of Chapter/Title 1. Although school site personnel must maintain appropriate records, it is both cost-efficient and helpful for a designated federal programs officer within a school district or shared among small school districts to either compile or check these data and reports before they are forwarded to the federal regulators or to their state designees. Additionally, it is helpful to the superintendent and board to maintain copies of such information at the central office so that immediate access is available for all schools in the district.

SBM AND CHAPTER 1

The impact of site-based management (SBM) on Chapter/Title 1 as well as other federal programs is that of empowering school staffs and administrators to try new processes and programs in order to better assure student achievement. Of course, the federal regulatory strictures will remain unless a waiver has been granted. However, the changing central office role with regard to SBM could, and in some cases should, be a causative factor in requests for waivers districtwide in order to facilitate innovation within the individual school and its programs. Knowledge of the law and Chapter/Title 1 regulations plays a crucial role in the efforts districts or schools may undertake to obtain waivers and to improve instruction and student learning outcomes.

FEDERAL PROGRAMS DEALING WITH DISABILITY

Both federal and state governments guarantee educational access for the handicapped. Additionally, legal cases at the state and national levels have set precedents for educational opportunity for students with disabilities. Issues surrounding provision of service include placement of students with disabilities identified under IDEA and P.L. 94-142 within the regular classroom with the provision of indirect services, mainstreaming of students, inclusion, and placement only in special education classes. It is applicable to students in K–12 education, ages 0–21.

Other federal laws that impact students with disabilities and the school and district are the Americans with Disabilities Act (ADA) and Section 504. Section 504, with its call for "reasonable accommodation," is applicable to students and to those who must provide the "reasonable accommodations" that must be made to allow students with diabilities to access education. Section 504 is applicable as well as to adults and employees of the district. ADA relates to the adults who come into the building, school, or district, that is, teachers, staff members, and patrons. The Americans with Disabilities Act focuses on employers and the issue of access for "otherwise qualified" individuals. It is important to note that Section 504 is applicable only where federal funds are received. It is rare for a public school not to receive public funds, and some private schools may receive some federal funding as well. Regardless of funding received, ADA is applicable to schools and to school districts, depending only on the number of employees within the school district. Again, there are few, if any, school districts that are so small as not to be covered by ADA and its requirements.

IDEA

Since teachers generally are not schooled in the intricacies of special education law, unless they are special educators, it is imperative that administrators have a knowledge of the law and its attendant regulations. Principals, with the notable exception of those who may either choose or be required to choose a course on the "exceptional child" during their certification training, tend to "pick up" information concerning special education through in-service and actual conferences and Educational Management Team (EMT) meetings. The EMT is the group of individuals—regular teachers, special education teachers, parents, administrators, other personnel as necessary, and sometimes the students themselves—who staff the special education students. To "staff" the student implies evaluation or reevaluation, placement, and the writing of or modifications to the Individual Education Plan (IEP) of the student. The other personnel who may be included are therapists and psychological examiners. Categories of students who may be included within special education programs are defined within the law itself.

The presence of a central office administrator who has the time and the knowledge and whose task it is to remain current with legal precedent and issues relative to special education is crucial. It is that individual and his or her staff, if any, who will respond to concerns, assist principals and teachers, and represent the school district in the event that a legal issue arises that must be addressed within the courts or at an administrative hearing by the state special education officer. Furthermore, the special education administrator is the individual within the school district who must ensure compliance with regulations relative to timelines, testing procedures, and correct completion of student IEP and testing protocols.

INCLUSION

In the past four to five years, several cases have arisen within the federal courts relative to the full inclusion of students with handicapping conditions in the regular classroom. Naturally, the possibility of full inclusion of students, particularly those who are medically fragile, has raised concerns among regular classroom teachers, the parents of students without disabilities, and in many cases, the parents of students with disabilities. It is understandable that such concerns exist. Since special education has been a fact of American education for more than 25 years, most regular teachers and indeed the parents of most children who are now in K–12 education have never taught or been taught in classrooms with such inclusion.

Inclusion represents an attempt to provide regular teachers the support services in their classrooms that are necessary to assist children with disabilities, to raise the quality of education for students with disabilities, to reverse the fragmentation of students' learning experiences that has resulted from "pullout programs," and to raise expectations for children with handicapping conditions (Podemski, Marsh, Smith, & Price, 1995, p. 23). With regard to inclusionary efforts, which in the minds of many represent a major reformation of special education, it is the role of the central administrator to foster collaboration among all teachers of the identified students. It is the role of the special education administrator to ensure the appropriate expenditure of federal funds to support the education of students, to assure that appropriate support services are brought to the inclusive classroom, and to provide for the training of teachers who will have "included" students within their classes. This will involve address to a range of new fiscal issues which has arisen as a direct result of inclusion (Parrish, 1995).

ADA AND SECTION 504 OF THE REHABILITATION ACT OF 1973

Section 504 addresses the civil rights enforcement of the 1973 Rehabilitation Act, which provides for rehabilitation services of all individuals. As previously noted, the 1973 Act provides for children in schools as well as for adults who may come into or work in schools. The Americans with Disabilities Act of 1990, on the other hand, guarantees individuals with disabilities equal opportunities in employment, public transportation, and public accommodations. This latter act refers to individuals who would be "otherwise qualified" to fill a position absent their disability and for whom "reasonable accommodations" may be made to ensure their opportunity to fill the position in question.

Inherent in the requirements attendant to Section 504 and ADA are continuing public notice of the fact that the school district does not discriminate on the basis of disability, and notice to employees of the same information. The responsibility of providing notice is, of course, the responsibility of the central administration as it impacts all schools and facilities owned or used by the school district. It is also a task of designated central office administrators to inform principals of the existence and exigencies of the law.

The concept of "reasonable accommodation" carries with it a heavy responsibility relating not only to instructional activities within a school district but also to modifications in facilities, in training materials, in job applications, and in work schedules to accommodate individuals with disabilities (Zirkel, 1992). For students, this includes modifications within class presentations and testing procedures. Again, it is the role of the central office administrators, usually the special education coordinators, to be knowledgeable about these requirements and to ensure that all affected teachers, administrators, and staff members are adequately educated as to their responsibilities under the law.

Section 504 also impacts student participation in extra-curricular activities. There is not a requirement that the disability of the individual not be considered but rather that the student must be otherwise qualified and must not be excluded only on the basis of his or her handicapping condition. A knowledgeable superintendent, central office staff, and principal can save the district possible costly litigation and/or "bad press" by educating teachers about these laws, their requirements, and their potential consequences. Additionally, the superintendent in tandem with school staff can ensure that all students, not only the student with a disability, receive maximal educational opportunities within the classes in which inclusion occurs.

FEDERAL PROGRAMS RELATIVE TO STUDENT WELFARE

The federal government has provided programs intended to enhance the welfare of students in the form of grants and legislation virtually since the inception of the country. As early as 1785, the Northwest Ordinance reserved land in every township for the maintenance of public schools. "In 1935, Public Law 320 was passed, authorizing the Secretary of Agriculture to purchase certain surplus agricultural projects and distribute them free of charge to schools which had school lunch programs" (Drake & Roe, 1994, p. 185). As a result of the popularity of this act with farmers and school patrons, a 1943 school indemnity plan was adopted (p. 186) by which the Department of Agriculture provided reimbursement to schools for the purchase of specific agricultural products. The next iteration of nutritional concern for students in school was the 1946 School Lunch Act, which is still operative (with minor variations from state to state). In 1966 the Child Nutrition Act was passed. This legislation provided for congressional funding of school lunch programs for needy children and for federal supplement of costs for school lunches in general. The Child Nutrition Act works in tandem with the 1946 act. In 1975, an additional piece of legislation, Public Law 94-105, was passed, which provides for school breakfast programs for students who qualify. Additional programs administered through these acts and by school districts are nutrition education and summer food services for children.

The provision of lunch and breakfast for students under these acts and federal regulations is based on family income. Depending on family income, students pay nothing (that is, they qualify for free lunch), pay a reduced price, or pay the usual district charge to students. The usual charge is in itself a reduced price, as costs are predicated on the use of USDA commodities at least in part and are supplemented with federal funds. The object, of course, is to benefit students. To that end, very specific nutritional and serving guidelines are provided to the schools for use in preparation and serving of school lunches and breakfasts.

Once again, the role of central office administrators is crucial, not only in terms of familiarity with these acts and their attendant regulations but also in terms of training for school cafeteria workers, dieticians, and administrators. While knowledge of requirements is essential, knowledge of conditions or constraints is also quite important. For example, school districts are not to contemplate making a profit from school lunch programs. There are requirements that even if students do not want certain items which comprise a school lunch, those students must take the full lunch and simply leave undesired items on the tray. There is a prohibition regarding these leftover items as well. Teachers may not take items that students chose not to eat even if the items are offered, but must allow them to be thrown away. Additionally, schools may not sell items, such as soft drinks and candy, in competition with the lunch program at any period of the day.

The school business manager, or the superintendent in small districts, must be able to make appropriate decisions relative to whether school kitchens are centralized or sited at schools or whether food services should be contracted out to some other entity. These functions and decisions concerning facilities, staffing, menus, purchasing, warehousing food, and budgeting are dependent on the central office. Even with school site management, the principal has neither the time nor the expertise to address all of these issues even though correct completion of free and reduced lunch forms and records maintenance are crucial at the school site. Additionally, as with many districtwide functions, there is efficiency and often there is monetary savings in central office coordination.

In recent years, the guidelines for a balanced meal and requirements for various food type combinations for student meals have changed. The federal government doubtless will continue these changes in the future. Although changes in student food programs may not be called "reform" by many, they are nonetheless important and must receive appropriate attention from central office staff and appropriate school-based personnel.

ROLES IN LARGE AND SMALL SCHOOL DISTRICTS

Whether a school district is large or small and regardless of its demographics, the role of central office remains important even in an era of reform, restructuring, and school-based management. There are many programs that are better managed from the central level. Staff development and support for principals take on crucial dimensions in districts in which SBM has added responsibilities and final accountability to the principals' already full plates.

In large districts, there may be one individual who oversees federal programs that relate to curriculum and instruction. There is generally another individual, often working with support staff, who manages the food programs. This is true whether the district uses a central kitchen or maintains kitchens at schools. In large districts as well there is frequently a grant writer whose tasks are to keep abreast of federal grant requests for proposals (RFP), to contact appropriate persons, to oversee the grant application process, and/or to write grants himself or herself.

In smaller districts, it may be the responsibility of the school superintendent and business manager to coordinate both federal curricular programs and school food programs. Generally, grant writing and management one also within their purview although they may be delegated to a committee of teachers, school administrators, or an assistant superintendent if such a person exists within the district.

FEDERAL FUNDING FOR THE FUTURE

There is a trend in federal funding, begun with the mid-term elections of 1995, of providing federal money in the form of block grants. Block grants cover a wide range of somewhat related programs and projects. For example, a block grant in the area of disability may provide support for programs, special staff, equipment, materials, transportation, special services, staff development, gifted students, and so forth. Generally, usage of block grant money is not strictly prescribed as long as the grant money and the project it funds bear a reasonable relationship with the general funding area. It is not usual for block grant money to be appropriated on a per-cost unit basis. A lump sum is appropriated from which districts must decide allocations and supplement with state and local money as deemed necessary.

Block grants are to be distinguished from categorical grants, which address specific and discrete areas of educational involvement. For example, categorical money may be appropriated just for gifted and talented programs to be allocated on a per-pupil basis. In this case, the amount that must be spent from federal funds per pupil is specified.

The trend toward block grants, on the one hand, gives a reasonable amount of freedom to districts in terms of the distribution of funds within the specific programs covered by the grant appropriation. On the other hand, however, the money appropriated in block grants may not cover the costs of meeting programmatic or pupil needs as categorical funds tend to do because block grant money is not allocated on a per-pupil basis. Programs and services for students tend to cost districts more from local funding. This trend does not appear to represent a passing aberration. School district administrators and school boards must factor the new costs into their budgeting and planning processes for the foreseeable future.

REFERENCES

Drake, T. L. & Roe, W. H. (1994). *School business management.* Boston: Allyn & Bacon.

Miller, J. A. (June 21, 1995). New title I law will bring shift in funding to schools this fall. *Education Week.* pp. 1,27.

Parrish, T. B. (Fall, 1995). Fiscal issues related to the inclusion of students with disabilities. *CSEF Brief,* 7. Palo Alto, CA: American Institutes for Research.

Podemski, R. S., March, G. E., Smith, T. E. C., & Price, B. J. (1995). *Comprehensive administration of special education.* Englewood Cliffs, NJ: Merrill.

Zirkel, P. (1992). A checklist for determining legal eligibility of ADD/ADHD students. *The Special Educator.* 8 (3):3–4 Horsham, PA: LRP Publications.

CHAPTER 5

The State and the School District

As the single largest source of funding in many districts and the source of the existence of virtually all school districts, the impact of the state and the necessity for understanding state laws and regulations are undeniable.

STATE regulations and funding are pivotal in most school districts. Although the federal government does play a significant role in school district functions by virtue of some funding and regulations in several key programmatic areas, it is the state that provides about 35–40% of the funding for school district operations, on average. Of course there are some districts that, because of their local wealth, receive less state funding and some that, because of their relative lack of local wealth, receive a greater percentage of their funding from the state. As was noted in Chapter 1 of this text, in the state of Hawaii all district funding that is not federal in origin comes from the state as there is only one school district in Hawaii.

The state is, of course, the legal entity that created and regulates school districts and much of their activity. The state, embodied in the legislature, passes school finance law and determines such guidelines as the division of funds into personnel and other expenditures; the amount of required base funding for texts, specific programs, and certified salaries; and curricular standards for the schools within that state. Generally, it is the state school officer, variously called the Director of the Department of Education, Commissioner of Education, or Chief State School Officer, who, with his or her staff, is empowered to write regulations attendant to the legislative acts and to enforce state policy relative to schools.

In many states, there are laws concerning home schooling and charter schools. These laws also are managed and records are maintained by the state department of education. Mandated state standardized testing is also within the bailiwick of the state department. The state department staff is responsible for writing policy and regulations with regard to mandatory school attendance, the maintenance of records, and the regulation of expenditures, as well as for ensuring accountability for state funding received by school districts.

STATE FUNDING AND GOVERNANCE

Among the programs funded through the state in addition to the general funding program, which is often called the Minimum Foundation program or the state Equalization Program, are categorical programs such as vocational education, compensatory education, and gifted and talented education. The educational dimensions in which the state is involved "fall into at least five general categories: instructional program, certification of personnel, facilities, standards, financial support, and nonpublic schools" (First, 1992, p. 154). In each of these areas, the district, and consequently its board, superintendent, and central office administration, must be knowledgeable and answerable to the state school officer, the legislature, the appointed or elected state board of education, and through them, the governor.

In either case, whether the state board and the state school officer/commissioner are elected or appointed by the governor, partisan politics may enter into the equation. Consequently, it is important not only for the superintendent and his central office staff to be knowledgeable of the state laws and regulations but also to understand the possible or potential consequences of certain regulations and to lobby with the legislature, with the governor, and, insofar as practical and possible, with members of the state board, many of whom are not educators.

Of course, it is the state board of education that sets certification guidelines for teachers and administrators, although these are monitored and records are kept by personnel in the state department of education. It is through the state department of education that an individual or a district may obtain a waiver from legal requirements in terms of class size, curricular offerings, and programmatic implementation. The state acts as the agent overseeing special education and gifted education even though each of these is defined within federal law. The state is the primary agent for dissemination of Chapter 1 funds and other compensatory money. The state department of education or education commission, as applicable, monitors the expenditure of these funds and the educational results of programs as well as expenditures on a district-by-district basis. This is the accountability role of the state.

AREAS OF STATE IMPACT ON SCHOOLS

State government controls school districts and directs their operation and continued existence far more than does the federal government. It is often the state which is the fiscal and evaluational agent for federal programs. In fact, in many states, the state government issues comparative report cards showing district-by-district progress fiscally, in regard to student attendance, completion rates, and academic achievement.

During the current stage of reform, address to the ongoing operations of schools and change itself is made more difficult for the school district since the state too is facing changes and reform. In fact, national changes have caught states and school districts in the middle, between those who wish education to remain as it has always been and those who are calling for major revision and restructuring within the educational milieu of our public schools. "Widespread resistance to local government spending on education suggests that Americans have diminishing confidence . . . that public authorities can forge effective compromises among divergent views" (Steiner, 1994, p. 5). An almost constant barrage of criticism leveled at schools since 1983 has placed superintendents, school boards, and central office appointees in a precarious position.

PRESSURES FACED BY STATES

On the one hand, the states are under pressure from the National Governors' Association through the Association of Chief State School Officers to enhance teacher accountability, improve student achievement, restructure schools, and ensure by virtue of a new series of examinations that teachers and administrators are appropriately certified and qualified for the positions they hold. On the other hand, the United States Department of Education (USDOE) is involved in several initiatives surrounding the National Goals, or Goals 2000 as they are sometimes called. Initiatives include the commissioning of the writing of national standards in core curricular areas. (As of this writing, standards have been completed in mathematics, English and language arts, and social studies, albeit with some controversy in the latter field.) The USDOE, through some of its appointed panels such as the national assessment in education panel (NAEP), and some of its departments such as the Office of Eductional Research and Improvement (OERI), is seeking ways to ensure accountability by schools and districts. Among the possibilities are the implementation of a national curriculum and the development of a national examination.

Precedents for the national examination exist among the states both in the form of K–12 exit examinations and in some states, a college exit examination. Precedent for national standards has existed in many states for some time in the form of state curricular standards/frameworks.

CENTRAL OFFICE RESPONSE TO CHANGE

The difficulty for central office administrators during this time of change at many levels is whether to initiate change at all. If the federal government is going to mandate change and if the state, the primary external force in school district management, is developing new regulations and expectations, the possibility looms large that change will follow change without the time necessary for constituents and employees to absorb and respond appropriately to those changes. Central administrators can ill afford to give into this temptation, however. There are specific policies systems that must be operative and constantly improved in every school system regardless of external demands for change or laws requiring that change.

Restructuring is difficult at best. That difficulty is compounded when the directions and directives relative to change come not from within or from the constituency represented by the school district but rather from the state. The role of central office administrators is impacted initially in any change. In the first place, there is dependence on the central administrator to understand the implications of laws and regulations promulgated by the state so that these central administrators can "run interference" for school site leaders and their staffs.

Second, the movement from a traditional role as overseer to that of facilitator is difficult for some central office administrators. That difficulty is compounded in circumstances in which school principals and teachers begin to exercise their newfound freedom by challenging virtually everything their former central office supervisors have to say. Tewel (1994), in an interesting article in *The Executive Educator,* writes of the feelings of confusion and loss experienced by central office administrators: "Many, feeling the sand shift beneath their feet, worried that their power had been eroded while their responsibilities had increased" (p. 31). Indeed, it is probably harder to create the trappings of consensus in a district that is restructuring, but trappings have never been equivalent to consensus in any district. With shifts in "perceived power" and sometimes in authority, teachers, patrons, and principals now are speaking out. At least in the process of consensus building, all, including central office administrators, will both see and hear agreement on the changes, whether mandated by the state or evolved and implemented by the district.

THE MORE THINGS CHANGE

In spite of changes forthcoming from national and state initiatives, some key components of state-mandated school procedures will not change, and the role of central office administrators will therefore remain constant. State funding of programs, whether by categorical allocation (per student in the program) or by means of block grant, will remain a constant for the foreseeable future. School district administrators, specifically those in the central office, will maintain the responsibility to apply for resources based on data gathered relative to student participation in compensatory education, gifted and talented programs, special education, vocational education, transportation, and so forth. Allocation of such resources among the schools and assurance of compliance with state and federal regulations will be a consistent central office responsibility in conjunction with the school administrators and identified school staff. Final accounting and accountability with regard to funding and data gathering relative to student achievement on a school-by-school and districtwide basis will continue to be within the realm of central office responsibility.

Staff development and the development of policy reflective of changes which may be made at the state level are ongoing tasks for the superintendent and his or her staff. Providing continuous educational growth for the central office staff assigned these responsibilities and maintaining access to experts who can facilitate professional growth among the district staff members is imperative because it relates to potential changes required in policy to reflect state and federal expectations regarding education. As Tewel (1994) aptly put it, the central administrator in times of change will need to be available to all constituencies (including appropriate state liaisons), listen with empathy, and be willing to bypass old channels of authority in order to find new solutions (p.

34) or approaches to change and the change process. Indeed, restructuring, whether internally initiated or influenced by new state initiatives, involves the evolution of new roles and relationships with the final goal being that of improving employee performance and student achievement (Sashkin & Egermeier, 1992). In a sense, however, the new roles are those which progressive educators have sought to establish and to fill throughout the history of American education.

ACTION RESEARCH

An orderly and effective change process can only be achieved when central office administrators and, through their modeling and efforts, all personnel in a school district employ action research as a major and important tool in their change efforts. In other words, school districts must develop the capacity to solve problems themselves (Sashkin & Egermeier, 1992, p. 10). Based in solid research, sound data, and a well-developed knowledge base of good professional practice, site-based management can give both power and authority in decision making to the lowest possible level, that is, to the level closest to the student himself or herself, namely the classroom teacher. Absent such research, data, and knowledge, all power and authority essentially remain in the hands of central office administrators. Ironically, in districts in which capacity is lacking in the classrooms and at the school site for informed decision making, it is often lacking at the central office and among board members as well.

In an era of change and with pressure from the states in terms of licensure of certified staff, curricular frameworks, and funding, it is the informed data-based decision making of school districts that is most likely to persuade legislators and state school board members to grant waivers and/or to slow or increase the pace of change. Kathy Jervis and Joseph McDonald (1996) note in *Kappan* that tools for maintaining a focus on the student while also adopting and using the mandated standards-based teaching include knowing the theory of networking. If such approaches work for teachers, they can work for central office administrators as well.

Central office administrators may gain much by spending more time in schools to ensure that finances are supporting programs as intended and to verify that programs in place do in fact assist teacher and students in reaching the intended achievement results. Ideas may be shared as well by teachers with the central office administrator who can share those ideas in turn at other school sites (Jones, 1990). Such visits also enhance administrator credibility when the administrators works with teachers, patrons, school administrators, or state department of education employees relative to school change and improvement. Jones notes that "the foundation for the best and quickest improvement" (p. 78) is in the monitoring of schools and the provision of immediate feedback.

However, for long-term change, action research is best. In order to do this well, training must be provided to school staffs. Central office administrators, starting with the superintendent, may need such training as well. If done well, however, action research is central to the decentralization of schools and the movement to a facilitating role for central office administrators. Action research implies that each program or change made is preceded by the gathering of appropriate data that clearly demonstrates where the district is and what the strengths or weaknesses of the program might be prior to the contemplated change. Subsequent to implementation of changes in programs, processes, or procedures, data are continuously gathered, both qualitative and quantitative, in order to track progress or lack thereof so that definitive information is available with regard to the quality of programs and their fiscal efficiency in helping the district fulfill its mission and in assuring that student needs are met in line with state mandates and district policy.

REFERENCES

First, P. F. (1992). *Educational policy for school administrator.* Boston: Allyn & Bacon.

Jervis, K. & McDonald, J. (April 1996). Standards: The philosophical monster in the classroom. *Phi Delta Kappan,* 77(8):563–169.

Jones, R. R. (May 1990). Out of the ivory tower and into the schools. *Educational Leadership.* pp. 77–78.

Sashkin, M. & Egermeier, J. (October 1992). *School change models and processes: A review and synthesis of research and practice.* Working paper. ERIC: ED351757.

Steiner, D. M. (1994). *Rethinking democratic education: The politics of reform.* Baltimore: The Johns Hopkins University Press.

Tewel, K. J. (March 1994). Central office blues. *The Executive Educator.* pp. 31–35.

CHAPTER 6

Central Office Instructional Leadership: Curriculum Development and Supervision

> Although curriculum is crucial to the educational enterprise, the focus of
> central office administrators is often on day-to-day problems. The chapter
> describes the appropriate central office role.

WHEN Robert Carlson (1996), in his text *Reframing & Reform,* writes of
changes in educational practice in contemporary society and schools, he
distinguishes among restructuring, reform, and site-based management.
Carlson sees reform as a broad concept that although called for nationally, occurs in school districts and "seems to rise and fall with political
causes and perceived failings of the public schools" (p. 202). School restructuring, which may be a component of reform, "comes in many
forms" (p. 203) and has multiple dimensions. School-based management is or may be viewed as one form of school restructuring. Carlson's
definitions provide a significant clue to the relative roles of central office
administrators and other personnel and school site administrators, teachers, and staff as they relate to curriculum and instruction.

In this chapter and Chapter 7, these concepts will be fully fleshed out
so that the reader may develop an understanding of the directions reform
is taking relative to the teaching of students. Chapters 1 through 5 addressed primarily structure, process, and support functions within the
central office. Now we must turn our attention to the real role of education, namely the preparation of students to assume their places as educated citizens of a democratic society.

The current call for increased accountability on the part of educators is
a direct reflection of public and governmental concern relative to not
only the achievement of students in our schools but also to their behavior
while in school and subsequent to completing school. Youth culture,
violence, the use of illegal substances, and crime in general have gener-

ated a debate within the nation and within schools about the relative importance of teaching values. The much discussed decline in SAT scores has led members of the public and the press to bemoan student achievement as measured by standardized tests. The writings of authors such as Ravitch (1983), Hirsch (1987), and Bloom (1987) raise serious questions about the quality of the curriculum and instruction provided within American schools. Questions also have arisen and continue to arise about the quality of school leaders, teachers, and curriculum offerings themselves. Proposals for change include year-round school, new methods of sorting children for educational purposes (e.g., changes in organizational patterns, such as grade assignments housed in individual building) and alternative placements such as charter schools, privatized schools, and home schooling. (When the word *privatized* is used in relation to schools, we are speaking not of private or parochial schools but of schools taken over by "for profit" businesses such as Whittle's Edison schools or Educational Alternatives Inc. (EAI), which has operated in East Hartford, Connecticut, and continues to work in the Baltimore, Maryland, public schools.

Addressing these concerns is crucial in public schools. However, the best response may be improvement in the quality of the curriculum delivered and in the instructional methodology used. These improvements or changes must take place in classrooms with the support of principals and of central office personnel. The response to calls for greater accountability, which is necessary, cannot be a "wait and see" attitude on the part of educators because in that case legislatures and the national government would step in and impose standards and assessments to measure student learning. The appropriate response to calls for greater accountability is assumption of that accountability and demonstrable improvement in student achievement outcomes not only while students are in school but also when they enter the marketplace.

The focus and responsibility of educational leadership relative to curriculum must be:

- planning the curriculum
- educating staff and the public
- developing and packaging the curriculum and associated materials
- preparing teachers for curricular presentation (teaching)
- supervising and supporting teachers through the work of central office administrators and school site managers
- curricular maintenance and modification

PLANNING THE CURRICULUM

Curriculum planning is a process. In fact, curriculum is process-oriented. Although there are certain constants within the curriculum, such as English/language arts, mathematics, science, and social studies, these subjects are to some degree in process themselves. For example, history is living, not only because it is made on a daily basis but also because with the ongoing discovery of new materials and information, historians frequently revise historical interpretation. Science, of course, is constantly changing. The same is true of literature and the language we speak. As new discoveries are made, events occur, and new writings are published, schools are expected to reflect these within the curriculum. Imbedded within this expectation is the belief that teachers should be prepared to present the new materials with confidence and competence. Of course, the ability of teachers to teach new ideas and to present new materials is directly related to the continuing professional growth of those teachers.

The planning of curriculum for schools and districts must necessarily include relevant state standards and curricular requirements. It seems that national standards must also be considered in light of the national goals and national standards that have been developed and disseminated. Although the latter are not now required, there is a reasonable possibility that they will be mandated if a national curriculum is proposed and adopted in the foreseeable future either under the aegis of the USDOE or the National Governors' Association.

Even in light of state and national curricular guidelines, the teachers within a school district must be comfortable not only with the curriculum adopted in the school district and with relevant state curriculum frameworks but also with the materials, strategies, and concepts that are part of that curriculum. Consequently, it is crucial that teachers be included in both the curriculum planning and development processes.

The local campus [is] the focal point of most educational program planning and delivery" (Candoli, 1991, p. 62). This is true whether or not teachers are involved in the planning. Therefore, to ensure continuity of curriculum across schools and from grade to grade, those teachers who are expected to deliver the curriculum must be involved in the planning process. Of course, compliance with district policy and state law is a given in both the planning and curriculum delivery processes. A crucial role of central office administrators is to ensure such compliance. Additionally, the concept of "teacher buy in" to the curriculum, that is, ensuring that the taught curriculum is indeed the district curriculum, is crucial to student learning. It is only when teachers are involved in the process and empowered to make curricular decisions that such assurance is forthcoming.

CENTRAL OFFICE FACILITATION

Facilitation of the planning processes should be within the purview of the central office staff. In medium-sized and large school districts, this work is generally done by curriculum supervisors who are specialists in the particular curricular area or field. These supervisors may be housed in the district administration building or at school sites. In smaller districts, a lead teacher under the auspices of the superintendent or an assistant superintendent will often coordinate the planning process. (Frequently the lead teacher and other teachers who assist with planning and curriculum writing are placed on extended contracts or paid additional stipends in order to "buy time" for them to work. Such an arrangement is less costly than hiring a full-time supervisor, and it may work well in smaller school districts.) One caveat, however, is that those who are involved in curriculum development must have a desire to be so involved, not for the money or the release time but because of an abiding interest in curricular improvement and student learning. It is true that one cannot empower an individual who does not want to be empowered.

In some states, small school districts engage in joint planning through the offices of an educational cooperative. The educational cooperative plays an important role in terms of district support, particularly in the areas of curriculum and staff development. The cooperative may also enhance the possibility that the small district with a limited budget can provide the full range of services needed by all students within the district. Small districts typically cannot afford to hire supervisory staff for specific curricular areas. Cooperative arrangements allow districts to contribute dollars to a central agency, the coop, based on a per-pupil assessment or the number of schools within the district. The educational cooperative then employs a director and curriculum specialists who work to assist all districts that are cooperative members. Generally, cooperatives are geographically based, that is, they operate with the schools within a particular county or region of a state.

Whichever arrangement exists relative to a district, the work of curricular planning entails development of strategies, identification of resources, decision making with regard to specific concepts and skills to be taught, and the writing of learning objectives. Curriculum planning and writing are time-consuming and demanding tasks. Teachers must have not only ample time but also support to accomplish the tasks of curriculum planning and writing. Accordingly, the central office staff must ensure that teachers have space, materials, time, and the appropriate stipends, if work is done other than on regularly contracted days, to complete this task efficiently and with efficacy. If the work is to be completed within the school day, central administrators must provide substitutes for teachers.

The following model format is useful and may be adopted by school districts "as is" for use in curriculum writing. It is important that one easily understood format be adopted and used across the curriculum.

Objective to Be Taught		
Concepts	Skills Strategies	Materials/Resources

The format may be used for each objective to be taught. The alignment of concepts to be mastered by the student and applicable skills the student should learn, either thinking skills or other course-specific skills, can be clearly delimited for the teachers of the subject or unit. Additionally, suggested strategies for addressing the variant needs of students and materials or resources including, but not limited to, the adopted textbook may be listed for teacher assistance. Of course, lists of materials and resources recommended should be available within the school district and should be updated regularly.

CURRICULAR ARTICULATION

Curriculum planning should involve the articulation and development of key concepts and skills from grade to grade and subject, to ensure the reinforcement of those concepts and skills and to provide for growth by the student. Fenwick English (1992) notes that curriculum shapes the work of "teachers by focusing and connecting it as a kind of work plan in schools" (p. x). Alignment of that curriculum ensures not only that the curriculum is articulated across grade levels but also that it relates to testing. Growth is predicated on the increasing degree of difficulty of the particular concept as well as its increasing depth and breadth as the student matures intellectually and moves from grade to grade and subject to subject.

Additionally, the curriculum is to be mapped, that is, the location of concepts must be identified from course to course. Locating concepts and skills is a sound basis for ensuring that there are no knowledge gaps and that there is a relationship among and development of concepts through a student's educational career. Mapping also serves an important instructional role as it facilitates interdisciplinary teaching and learning by assisting teachers with cross-curricular planning and instruction.

TESTING AND THE CURRICULUM

When considering the use of standardized testing and teacher-made tests within schools, we must also consider the ways in which the developed and delivered curriculum is correlated with the concepts and skills that will be tested. This does not imply that teachers should have access to standardized test questions or that they should teach to the tests. Rather, the implication is that students and teachers are responsible for the mastery of certain concepts and skills within the taught classroom curriculum and the learned curriculum. (It is important to recognize that the taught and learned curriculum may not be coincident.) The taught and learned curricula reflect nationally recognized concepts and skills of importance in the case of standardized tests. Standardized tests are validated and have been tested for reliability as well. This is certainly one of the reasons why the public and the media tend to use standardized test results as a basis for their judgments relative to the quality of education in individual school districts and on a national level as well.

In the case of teacher-made testing, examinations will tend to reflect that which the teacher and student teach and learn, respectively, but absent alignment, it may not encompass that which is included in national testing. What is suggested here is that curriculum should be undergirded by a consideration of those concepts and skills that are tested on national instruments, regardless of the type of testing being used at a given time.

WRITING, PACKAGING, AND PRESENTING THE CURRICULUM

In addition to compliance with legislated state and national standards, the curriculum will reflect the priorities of the school board which, in turn, generally reflect the priorities of the school district community. Board policy will designate expectations with regard to curricular development, both process and conformity with the law. It is important that teachers who assist in the process of writing and packaging the curriculum understand these exigencies. Teachers can sometimes tend to focus attention on technique and on sustaining personal, and sometimes selfish, motives (Bruckerhoff, 1991), thereby leading to unsatisfactory results.

Selfish motives and personal interests have no place in the preparation of curriculum. The preparation of students is the goal and should be the focus of a school or class curriculum. Knowledge of subject or discipline content implies that the student can show an understanding of "ideas, theories, or perspectives considered central to an academic or professional discipline" (Newmann & Wehlage, 1995, p. 15). Consequently, the written curriculum must contain those ideas, theories, and perspectives that teachers are expected to teach and test.

Once the curriculum is written, it must be packaged and sent to the school board for approval. Packaging is important to both the board and the public. It includes not just the actual package (i.e., cover, binding, and so forth), but also the executive summary of the curriculum and an explanation as to the utility of the written curriculum. Such an explanation must include a discussion of the expected outcomes which will benefit students and the community by virtue of student mastery of the curriculum. Packaging is also important to teachers themselves. Each individual teacher must know that the written and board-adopted, mandated curriculum is within his or her ken and is appropriate for the students whom he or she teaches. Of course, the staff development and individual guidance offered by a supervisor, either the principal, the curriculum supervisor, or a mentor teacher, will be a major determining factor in teacher comfort level with the curriculum.

PREPARING TEACHERS FOR THE CURRICULUM

Teacher preparation for the curriculum is key. Change is not comfortable for most adults, a fact which adult learning theorists often mention. Consequently, what is done to prepare people for change may be the crucial component in the eventual acceptance of curricular modifications or a new curriculum. There are several components of such preparation which may be helpful to a central office practitioner who wants to prepare teachers for changes in the content they must teach. Among these are:

- holding cluster meetings to inform teachers of coming changes and to solicit their input prior to beginning the curriculum development work
- inviting teachers to volunteer to serve on the curriculum development team
- asking or selecting some teachers to review the work of the team as it progresses and to offer suggestions
- providing in-service for small clusters of teachers relative to content, strategies, skills, concepts, and expectations prior to implementation of the curriculum in the schools

Teachers who feel empowered and involved will generally work to ensure the success of projects, ideas, and curriculum. Teachers who are omitted from involvement often select a role of saboteur for themselves, a role in which many teachers are successful. Teachers who have opted not to be involved will generally observe this process and decide in light of ensuing events whether to support the saboteurs or to become late adopters of the curricular changes developed by the district and some of their colleagues. If the process of development and presentation has been efficacious, then most teachers will be supportive, as the process itself, and the roles played by central office staff and by other teachers will influence them in positive ways. That positive influence borne of appropriate task and human relationships in completion of the task provides the definition of efficacy (Carlson, 1996, p. 141).

From the perspective of the community, the teacher is one of the most powerful spokesperson for a school district or its programs. Therefore, it is crucial that teachers believe and feel that the programs offered within their classrooms and the district in general are of high quality and are meeting the needs of students. Teacher involvement is one very good way to ensure such communication with the community from teachers.

CURRICULUM SUPERVISION AND SUPPORT

When we speak of curriculum supervision and support, we are addressing the ongoing responsibility of school site and central office administrators to ensure that the curriculum that is written and adopted is implemented correctly. We are speaking of the need not only for monitoring but also for adjusting curriculum and strategies for delivering it in order to address unexpected problems and/or to meet the instructional needs of diverse groups of students.

Provision of such support implies that supervisors must be in classrooms, not only to see firsthand how teachers deliver the curriculum but also to teach it themselves in order to ascertain student responses to the curriculum and to identify areas of that curriculum that must be modified or enhanced. Supervision of curriculum is just that. To supervise curriculum is not to evaluate teachers; rather, it is to observe the curriculum being taught in order to identify content that must be more fully developed or explained. Supervision of curriculum means checking to ensure the alignment of curriculum to tests both by examining tested concepts and skills and by monitoring student performance. Supervision of curriculum implies that an effort is made to examine the articulation of the curriculum from course to course and throughout the educational years of the student. This supervision need not be done solely by central office administrators and principals; colleagues and teacher mentors may be involved in the process as well. In fact, it is suggested that such collegial relations be fostered and recognized within a restructuring school district, for they are not only efficacious but also efficient and demonstrate confidence in and recognition of the skills of teachers.

During this process, the tools used are observation, teacher and student interviews, and surveys of patrons and persons in the community who have dealings with students. The purpose of the latter surveys is to check to see if students are learning skills and content that will benefit them in the world of work and/or in higher education once they complete their years in the K–12 school setting.

Finally, such supervision implies that the supervisor and teacher are able to identify needed resources as well as resources that are no longer necessary or are outdated and therefore do not support the learning process. Supervisors may also identify particular teachers who are most successful in delivering the curriculum to students and garner strategies from these successful teachers to share with others who may be in need of some assistance or ideas for improving student mastery of subject matter within their classrooms.

CURRICULAR MAINTENANCE AND MODIFICATION

If the curriculum development and supervision processes within schools and within school districts are appropriately and effectively carried out, then maintenance of curriculum by updating materials and other resources should be cost-effective and efficient. Additionally, modification of the curriculum can be ongoing and will not be an onerous or expensive task. Teachers may elect to gain staff development continuing education units (CEUs) by virtue of their own classroom experiences, action research, attendance at professional growth activities, and collegial discussions. They may also do so by sharing these personal and professional growth experiences with others within the curriculum guides on which they may work either for stipends or for additional CEUs.

Curriculum development is a major responsibility of instructional leaders. Doubtless, central office administrators must take the lead, particularly in light of the fact that central office administrators generally have more time and opportunity to keep abreast of state and national level changes in regard to curriculum. Curriculum development and maintenance are responsibilities in which the whole school community has a stake. Therefore, it is within that whole school community that central office administrators may find support and willing assistance if they will ask for it and then facilitate the work and empower others to work with the processes involved in the development and maintenance of quality curriculum and resources to support that curiculum for the benefit of all students within the school district.

REFERENCES

Bloom, A. (1987). *The closing of the American mind.* NY: Simon and Shuster.

Bruckerhoff, C. (1991). *Between classes: Faculty life at Truman High.* New York: Teacher's College Press.

Candoli, I. C. (1991). *School system administration: A strategic plan for site-based management.* Lancaster, PA: Technomic Publishing Co., Inc.

Carlson, R. V. (1996). *Reframing & reform.* White Plains, NY: Longman Publishers.

English, F. W. (1992). *Deciding what to teach and test.* Newbury Park, CA: Corwin.

Hirsch, E. D. (1987). *Cultural literacy: What every American needs to know.* Boston: Houghton Mifflin Co.

Martusewicz, R. A. & Reynolds, W. M. (eds.) (1994). *Inside/out: Contemporary critical perspectives in education.* NY: St. Martin's Press.

Newmann, F. M. & Wehlage, G. G. (1995). *Successful school restructuring: A report to the public and educators.* Madison, WI: Center on Organization and Restructuring of Schools.

Ravitch, D. (1983). *The troubled crusade.* NY: Basic Books.

CHAPTER 7

Central Office Instructional Leadership: Personnel Development and Instructional Delivery Roles and Goals

The central office role as concerning personnel has traditionally been one of hiring, firing, and monitoring staff. Professional development delivered in a systematic fashion and based on assessed instructional needs represents a new and necessary approach to personnel functions aimed at ensuring student success.

CENTRAL office roles and responsibilities are more difficult and less clear as they relate to instructional delivery than as they relate to curriculum development and maintenance. However, they are absolutely clear relative to personnel development. A review of these roles and responsibilities is appropriate prior to delving into the changing relationships consequent to contemporary demands for reform and restructuring in schools.

INSTRUCTIONAL DELIVERY

The central office role in relation to instructional delivery is preponderantly supportive. This is not to imply that it is not a vital role, however. The primary responsibility for teacher evaluation and instructional observation, the clinical cycle, is and must be a key function of the school principal and assistant principals, if the principal has such support. Central office administrators will be responsible for the clinical supervision and evaluation of the school principal, however. The pattern of supervision, both summative and formative, for principals should both reflect and model that process employed by the building administrator in teacher supervision.

In regard to teacher assessment, the clinical supervision by the central office administrator will only be employed if the principal makes such a request of the subject matter supervisor or, in a large district, the appropriate assistant superintendent. In such a situation, the supervisor will observe and conference with the teacher with the principal present and after briefing the principal will provide assistance to the teacher. In the latter case, the central office supervisor will keep the principal apprised of the assistance provided and pertinent data from any observations conducted. The goal is to provide data so that the principal can continue to facilitate teacher growth and conduct pertinent summative evaluations at the appropriate time.

The superintendent should not be engaged in such a process, except as it relates to principal supervision in small districts, because it is important that the superintendent be able to maintain some objectivity should an employee termination recommendation of incompetence be brought forward by the principal. Such objectivity is important for two reasons: in order to be able to assist the principal with preparation of a case and for purposes of being able to formulate an appropriate and balanced recommendation to the board should a board hearing be necessary.

THE PERSONNEL FUNCTION

The personnel function is multifaceted. It encompasses identification and recruitment of potential employees, both teachers and support personnel; matching possible employees with positions for which they are qualified; conducting the interview process; facilitating the hiring process; and providing on-the-job in-service educational support for all staff. The responsibilities just described represent the positive side of the personnel function.

On the other hand, the personnel function may involve disciplining staff (both certified and noncertified); remediation of staff, as necessary and appropriate; recommendations for nonrenewal or termination of staff; conduct of the hearing process including all appeals; and a final recommendation to the superintendent and the board with regard to the continued employment of a teacher or other persons who have worked in the district. Most of these functions and those which were described as positive functions are conducted in tandem with the building principal. Principals ultimately are responsible for the hiring, development, monitoring, and, occasionally, the termination of their own staff members. The closer a school district moves toward defining and implementing school site management, the more the responsibility for these activities will devolve upon the shoulders of the principal. Of course, such movement toward school site management is in large part related to the understanding the superintendent and his or her central office administrators have of the concept and their willingness to empower others. Site-based management is not easily initiated. It takes thoughtful consideration, planning, and collaboration among central and school administrators.

Interestingly, there is no loss of either power or authority associated with the empowerment of principals and teachers. Not all school district personnel, either at the schools or in the central office, understand this, however. Consequently, unless the superintendent appropriately prepares and educates all staff as to what the vision of school site management (site-based management) entails, interesting yet damaging gamesmanship may emerge among and between principals and central office staff. Information blocking is one of the forms that such gamesmanship may take. Power is held by those who hold the information. Such informational control negatively impacts morale, performance, and productivity, however. It is the role of the superintendent to identify and stop such contending behaviors in order to ensure organizational health and informed decision making that involves all the necessary and appropriate stakeholders from schools and central office.

COLLABORATION AND TEAM BUILDING

As a component of the team building and empowerment that must be a feature of effective school districts, it is suggested that principals should be involved, at least as members of the interview team, in the selection of most central office personnel. This rule of thumb is particularly important when the central office administrator applicant is interviewing for a position that will provide direct support to the schools. Principals often know the specific expertise necessary for the development of and improvement of curricular programs and for the enhancement of teacher expertise in specific subject areas. They also are keenly aware of the type of support they and their colleagues need in order to work effectively as instructional and transformational leaders in their buildings. The interview process, in fact, can become the first step in collaboration.

It is the central office administrator who supports the principal as he or she tries to make changes in staffing patterns to benefit students or in methods for effective delivery of instruction. In site-based management, staffing assignments are varied from school to school and are dependent on an educated and informed assessment of that which will work best in the context of the needs of the students in that school and the school's goals for excellence. In other words, if the students cannot read, it is far more expeditious to use discretionary funds to hire additional reading teachers or aides than to continue to hire full-time art or music teachers.

This is not to say that art and music teachers are not important. An enterprising principal with assistance from astute central office administrators can arrange to "share" art and music teachers with other schools. This will ensure that state standards requiring such exposure for students are met while maximizing learning and remediation of students in the academic area of need, namely reading. If a cost-benefit analysis is conducted, the gains made by students under such a plan will more than justify the cost of the reading teacher. Additionally, the savings in terms of art and music will offset much of the reading teacher's associated cost. Finally, such a decision recognizes both the student need for cultural exposure and the crucial skills every student must possess in the area of reading.

ACTION RESEARCH

Central office specialists can support principals further by assisting them to pilot certain programs in order to ascertain the impact of the program prior to initiating it districtwide or on a schoolwide basis. It is the central office administrator, whether in a large, medium, or small district, who will assess the impact of such programs, jointly with principals, among schools in a district. Principals must be able to conduct action research to assess impact within their own programs, but they generally have little time to spend analyzing and evaluating programs in other schools within the district.

As noted by Wilson and Daviss (1994), "evaluators' repertoire of techniques enables them to design focused, detailed evaluations and draw accurate conclusions about most aspects of any educational program" (p. 149). Some currently practicing principals will not have the expertise to conduct action research. The central office administrator under the tutelage of the superintendent must facilitate this process of principals' learning action research. Wise superintendents will assure that such training is available to all who are responsible for programs and will seek to develop action research skills themselves. Such skills are not only a matter of efficiency and effectiveness from fiscal and student learning perspectives, they are also part and parcel of the superintendent's accountability for all that goes on within the instructional and support functions of the school district. Certainly, a superintendent who cannot assume such accountability cannot demand it of others.

For principals, action research and their own instructional and fiscal accountability relate to the fact that they have access to data (test scores and teacher-given grades), observational or clinical data, and general information with regard to teacher, student, and parent satisfaction and student learning outcomes. Central office supervisors have the opportunity and option to engage in productive dialogue with all interested stakeholders and to conduct surveys to garner information relative to programmatic success within and among schools. That information, supplemented by hard data, can provide a full picture of the value of programs, the general effectiveness of individuals working within them, and the adequacy of resources available to support the programs adopted within schools and the district itself. Such information should inform personnel and programmatic decisions and ensure improved educational opportunities for students and greater fiscal and educational accountability within the district itself.

In other words, such data can help the superintendent and board as well as all other line supervisors to make appropriate changes and reforms in the district not only in answer to public demands but also, more important, in response to demonstrated student and programmatic needs. Armed with appropriate data, decisions can be made relative to the closing or opening of schools, expansion or continuation of programs, purchase or retirement of equipment, and the termination of personnel, including teachers and principals, who are not doing their jobs. Schools can then focus on what really is their job, teaching students (Sykes, 1995).

PERSONNEL DEVELOPMENT

Frameworks for personnel development are to "develop the capacity of each school site . . . to effectively manage the educational direction of its school" (Gleason, Donohue, & Leader, 1996, p. 24). Support from central administration and the school board must include not only the traditional—that is, induction of new staff, maintenance or entry skills, development of traditional role-associated skills, and occasional brief exposure to new programs—but also a planned sequence of developmental in-service programs based on adult learning and deliberately focused on the district and school goals.

The undergirding premise is beautifully expressed in the often-cited quotation from Eric Hoffer (1982) in which he stated that "learners inherit the earth while the learned find themselves beautifully equipped to deal with a world that no longer exists" (p. 46). Hoy and Miskel (1996, p.

246) refer to the process of focused development in terms of inputs (effectiveness criteria such as fiscal resources, technology, and teacher quality), throughputs (harmony, culture, motivation, and process quality), and outcomes (achievement, job satisfaction, and performance quality). This is a form of community building as well as preparation for community membership for those who are and will be stakeholders in the new restructured community, which is the school and its surrounding district in light of restructuring and reform.

In this new community, the role of central office support of the schools in light of needed professional personnel development is to listen and to communicate clearly with the personnel who will receive training and assistance and with their supervisors, generally the principals. This task is made more difficult by virtue of the past experiences of all district personnel, namely those experiences in a more autocratic, "nonrestructured" district. Additionally, those tasks of two-way communication, which include listening, clarifying, reflection, and consensus building, are complicated by the simple fact that empowering others encourages the empowered to speak their minds. As noted by Kenneth Tewel (1994), who quoted a superintendent in a recent article, it is "much harder to gain consensus in a restructuring district. More people and more groups speak up" (p. 34). However, all personnel, be they certified or noncertified, must be convinced of the value of personal and professional development efforts and must understand the connectivity of such efforts to the vision of the school and district if they are to become willing participants and learners in professional growth.

Central office practitioners have a sort of balancing act to perform in light of the restructuring which was generally not necessary (or not acknowledged) in the days of autocratic administration. (It is doubtful that autocracy caused teachers or support staff to become truly engaged in professional growth, but at least lip service was paid to such commitment and involvement.) The balance is to be achieved among their own research-based focus on what needs to be done to ensure quality teaching and student learning; their respect for, and trust in, the expertise and commitment of the staff; and external demands placed upon the district and its schools by patrons and governmental entities.

PROFESSIONAL DEVELOPMENT AMID RESTRUCTURING

Within this framework, professional development programs that are effective, efficient, and focused must be offered to teachers and support staff alike. It is strongly suggested that these offerings relate to each other, that they reflect the best research and practice available, and that they offer benefits to the specific population the district and schools seek to serve. Fads have no place within a restructuring and reforming school system.

Programs of professional development, though tailored to the receiving population (be they teachers, administrators, or support staff), must share a common focus based on the common mission of the district and should reflect a core of common learning. Madelyn Hunter was correct when she spoke of the need for a common language among educators. Such a common language is absolutely essential among all who work within schools and with students. Finally, it must not be consultants who provide the ongoing training of staff.

Consultants have their place and may offer much to schools and districts on given occasions. Consultants, by definition, leave after presenting their ideas, and the issues of implementation and accountability remain within the district. It is far better to train in-house experts, namely teachers, administrators, and noncertified staff, who can provide continual training to colleagues and induction training to new employees. If this is not to be the case, the consultant should "sign on" for a long-term interactive relationship with the district in order to monitor new programs, continue training staff, and assume accountability for his or her own work in terms of learning and teaching results achieved within the district and/or the program being developed or refined.

There are three outstanding benefits of an arrangement whereby the district has in-house trainers. First, there is great empowerment inherent in having in-school or in-district experts. Second, individuals who are trainers and trainees alike develop appreciation for skills which each possess and a new spirit of collegiality. Finally, such a program is highly cost-efficient. The cost of in-depth training for individuals in particular skills and knowledge bases such as cooperative learning or mind mapping is generally less than the cost of sending several teachers for one or two days of introduction to the concepts, and the benefit is much greater and longer-lasting.

INSTRUCTION AS ART AND SCIENCE

Instruction is both an art and a science. Of necessity, the supervision of instruction must encompass both components as well. The art of instruction lies in the ability of the teacher to provide the climate necessary to maximize instruction and learning. It is found in the ability of that teacher to identify the learning styles, thinking styles, and modalities of students and to address them in all their diversity within each lesson. It is found in the construction of a lesson and the flow of instruction as the teacher motivates, focuses, leads, prods, and inspires the learner.

The science of instruction is in the factors identified in clinical supervision and in state or school district adopted observation checklists. It is to be found in the careful crafting of a lesson to include a set, an objective, questions, practice for the learner, modeling of the learning by the teacher, closure, and other aspects of the Program for Effective Teaching (PET) or other instructional models as appropriate to the lesson being presented.

All teachers can to a greater or lesser degree master the craft, that is, the science of teaching. However, the art of teaching is variable and is manifested not only in the acquired skills of the teacher but also in the heart of the teacher and the soul of his or her teaching. The art is only partly learned; much of it is innate just as perfect pitch is innate (but note that even a person without it can become a competent trained pianist).

If teaching is both an art and a science, so too is instructional supervision. Even with empowered teachers and principals, external collegial supervision is important as a motivator and as part of the growth process for every educator. The central office administrator and principal at the school site must see their roles, as supervisors in this way. The central office administrator not only may be supervising the teacher at the request of the principal but may also be assisting in the supervision of principals in all of their roles, including that of instructional supervisor. Certainly assistant superintendents and, in small districts particularly, the superintendent play a key role in the formative (instructional) and summative (evaluative) supervision of principals. Finally, the superintendent is an instructional supervisor for those who work within the support roles relative to instruction and curriculum in the central office.

In order to successfully restructure, assure student learning, and weather the calls for reform that swirl around education today, the teacher, principal, and central office administrators working together must become a learning community. "Educational administrators have a fundamental responsibility to administer the pursuit, exploration, construction, performance, and critique of meaning. . . . In this time of transition, a fundamental task of educational administrators is to infuse the traditional mission of the school with a new meaning" (Starratt, 1996, p. 69). A learning community is that culture in which people work with shared vision and acceptance of responsibility for each other as they work toward common goals and objectives. In education, of course, the common goals and objectives should be focused on maximizing the learning of students and the growth of those professionals who work with students so that the cycle of student achievement can be ongoing. Within that framework of community, administrators must exemplify that which they expect of others relative to power sharing, resource utilization, communication, personal standards of excellence, and using research-grounded information as a basis for decision making.

A further implication of community is that leadership is not relegated to those with the title "administrator" but involves, as Starratt (1996) suggests, teachers and all administrators, both central office and principals, engaging in a productive dialogue concerning "assessment of present practices and programs, design of new practices and structural arrangements, and a phased implementation of improvements" (p. 151). From an instructional and support perspective, the building of such a community is crucial. From the perspective of personnel management, the need for building community and utilizing the skills and expertise of teachers as partners and leaders in the instructional enterprise is essential if we are to keep our best and brightest teachers as well as develop new teachers. Several states have conducted surveys and ascertained that fully 20–33% of teachers leave the profession within their first five years. A North Carolina survey released recently showed that of the approximately one-third of teachers who left within the first five years, 44% had been in the top quarter of their college classes (Ponessa, 1996, p. 3).

ROLES AND GOALS FOR INSTRUCTIONAL IMPROVEMENT

Within the personnel function is not only the supervision role of administrators but also the hiring, firing, and placement of personnel. Support of and consultation with principals and teachers should inform this role as it does the clinical and developmental work of the districts. From a central office administrative perspective, this may be the newest role and the most difficult adjustment. The implication is not that screening of applicants, checking of credentials, and initial interviews ought not to take place in the central office. The fact is that principals and the teachers who teach in specific schools are the most knowledgeable concerning what is needed in the way of knowledge base, skills, experience, and even thinking styles to build the program and enhance delivery of curriculum.

Just as appropriate school staff members are to be involved in the selection of school site colleagues and principals, so too should teachers and principals be involved in the selection process from which central office supervisors are recommended for employment. In a strong school and system culture, not only are values and goals shared, but tasks for the accomplishment of work are shared also. Among those shared areas of work would be the participative decision making relative to hiring recommendations by those who have a vested interest in the position and the induction process by which new hires at any level are invested in the vision and goals of the school, program, and/or district.

The roles played by educators, both staff and line, and the goals they share are really the major arbiters of whether or not changes are made in the development of curriculum and in instructional delivery. Beyond that, the roles played and the goals shared are crucial in the productive growth and achievement of students. In an era of reform, one in which the public and the legislators are calling for alternatives to public education, including charter schools and home schooling, it behooves central administrators, particularly the superintendent and through him the board, to ensure the involvement, investment, and excellence of all personnel in a school district. Such involvement, which implies empowerment, must begin at the time of the initial hiring experience and continue until that teacher or administrator or support person is no longer officially employed by the school district. Change takes time. Excellence does not occur in one day. The high achievement of one class of students is not a guarantor of the high achievement of all classes of students. To make such change and to ensure its productive continuation, all district employees and stakeholders must be fully vested partners in the educational enterprise, with each working to support the other and for the students. In no way is the central administration giving up either its power or its authority, but rather it is governing "by design" (Starratt, 1996, p. 134), a design that facilitates change by allowing the central administrator to be used by the schools and engages schools and central office as a team with complementary roles for each member and identical game plans. This membership on the team is important for recognition, acheivement, and responsibility. All of these are motivators which, according to the theory of Hertzberg (1987), would add to the productivity and quality of the work of the teacher, administrator, and central office administrator.

LEGAL ISSUES AND IMPLICATIONS

If all vested parties are to be participants in the major processes of personnel and instructional function within the district, then all must be aware of the legal issues and of the implications of their involvement. Among the legal issues are confidentiality with regard to performance evaluation and personnel items in general. Items that are accessible to the public are only those covered under the Freedom of Information Act as it has been legislated in the various states. Additionally, before anyone participates in the hiring process, it is crucial that there be an understanding of the parameters of the interview process, namely which questions may be asked and which questions are impermissible.

Recruitment responsibilities for each individual within the team will and should be clearly delimited within district policy. Guidelines within district procedures must also exist relative to the induction and development process for new and continuing employees. Earlier mention of the need for some sort of clearly delineated and focused staff development that addresses the mission and goals of district and schools alike must be in place. This ensures that everyone has all of the skills and knowledge necessary to perform the educational tasks and that these skills are continuously updated.

Job deletion and addition justification are ongoing issues in most schools as districts. With the movement toward site-based management, principals and their staffs will be increasingly engaged in efforts to redesign staffing to meet learning and teaching needs unique to the school. Although the intent of school site management is to provide the school with a relatively free hand to hire and assign staff to maximize student learning, fiscal and certification issues must also be addressed. These are best addressed with the counsel and support of central office administrators. In the event that a waiver might be required relative to state standards, it is the central office supervisor who will doubtless assist with garnering the necessary support and completing the paperwork appropriately. It is the assistance and monitoring of the central office supervisor that will ensure that subsequent reports to the state and federal agencies are in compliance with regulations. (This, of course, is of great assistance to the principal.)

Additional legal areas in which central office administrators must have expertise are due process, evaluation (most states have a designated instrument and/or procedure), Act 504, Americans with Disabilities Act (ADA), and issues regarding discrimination. The last set of issues may focus on allegations of discrimination ranging from age to gender to race, as well as discrimination on the basis of a handicapping condition. District administrators, and indeed, principals, should have some knowledge about contract law, which involves "offer and acceptance, legally competent parties, consideration, legal subject matter, and agreement in a form required by law" (Webb, Greer, Montello & Norton, 1987, p.

129). Tort law, with an emphasis on liability issues—particularly in relation to a possible breach of the duty of supervision for principals and the duties of supervision and instruction for teachers—must also be understood. Finally, some understanding of agency and issues surrounding immunity for school employees in the particular state must be available through the offices of one or more central office administrators. Many districts both large and small keep legal counsel on retainer. In fact, some districts have an attorney as a permanent staff member. In that case, the attorney will often act as a labor relations lawyer in the case of grievances filed against the administration or in the event that an issue is taken to fact finding or arbitration. The latter occurrence generally only happens in districts in which there is a union or a teachers' association that has a professional negotiations agreement or contract with the school board. (Of course, such a contract, once adopted by the board, supersedes policy and is tantamount to law.)

Although it is expected that principals should have knowledge of these areas, that may not be generally true. Although most principals have had the benefit of a school law course and will therefore know something about torts and contracts, the depth of knowledge that may be necessary in some situations may not exist for many school leaders.

Specific expertise on the part of central office administrators, particularly those who deal with personnel and student disciplinary issues, is critical. The district's attorney may not always be available at the time at which an issue arises nor may the constant calling of an attorney be fiscally wise. Consequently, in this litigious society, central office expertise with regard to common legal issues is a key component of support for school site managers.

REFERENCES

Gleason, S. C., Donohue, N. & Leader, G. C. (January 1996). Boston revisits school-based management. *Educational Leadership.* (pp. 24–27).

Hertzberg, F. (1987). *In: The great writings in management and organizational behavior.* Boone, L. E. & Bowen, D. D. (eds.) pp. 168–185.

Hoffer, E. (1982). *Between the devil and the dragon: The best essays and aphorisms of Eric Hoffer.* NY: Harper & Row.

Hoy, W. K. & Miskel, C. G. (1996). *Educational administration* (5th ed.). NY: McGraw-Hill.

Ponessa, J. (June 19, 1996). High teacher attrition grabs attention in N.C. *Education Week.* 15(39):3.

Starratt, R. J. (1996). *Transforming educational administration: Meaning, community and excellence.* NY: McGraw-Hill.

Sykes, C. J. (1995). *Dumbing down our kids: Why American children feel good about themselves but can't read, write, or add.* NY: St. Martin's Press.

Tewel, K. J. (March 1994). Central office blues. *The Executive Educator.* pp. 31–35.

Webb, L. Dean, Greer, J. T., Montello, P. A., Norton, M. S. (1987). *Personnel administration in education.* Columbus, OH: Merrill Publishing Co.

Wilson, K. G. & Daviss, B. (1994). *Redesigning education.* NY: Henry Holt and Company, Inc.

CHAPTER 8

Special Programs for Special Needs

Since the passage of such legislation as IDEA, ADA, and Section 504, the teachers and administrators in school districts have been directly engaged in the education of students with handicapping conditions. The call for inclusion has added another dimension to the education of pupils. Populations of migrant, homeless, and health-impaired students now confront educators with new challenges as well.

SPECIAL programs for special needs students and their staff are crucial to the success of education within schools and districts in this era of change and reform. As noted in Chapter 4, in which federal programs were discussed, there are several programs for special needs students that must be managed and led within a school district regardless of the size of that district. Some of these programs are federally funded. Others may be funded only by the state. Some are identified in federal legislation but are funded from state coffers. In this chapter, each type of program and its funding will be reviewed in light of reform, restructuring, and leadership issues.

SPECIAL EDUCATION AND EDUCATORS

When the average educator considers the term *special needs students,* generally his or her thoughts turn to special education. This is true because for some twenty-plus years, special education has been a part of the educational lexicon and of educational practice. In fact, anyone who has come to teaching in public education since 1975 has never taught in a situation in which special education was not part and parcel of the school operations. Consequently, as legal precedent changes and calls for variation in special education practice are heard, many teachers and administrators alike are reluctant to make changes that might place "special" students in regular classes for longer periods of time or for the entire school day. (This concern is not unique to educators. Parents of students, both those identified as in need of special education services and students who are not so identified, often voice concern about the impact of integration or inclusion on the education of their children.)

In order to understand this reluctance, we must examine the special education categories, some trends in special education, and teacher preparation for addressing the diverse needs of students. Since the passage of Public Law (P.L.) 94-142 in 1975, as amended by IDEA (discussed below), the public schools have had special classes for students who have been identified as having specified disabilities. Among the disabilities listed in the law are mental retardation, learning disabilities, serious emotional disturbance, speech or hearing disability, and multiple disabilities. Under the law, students so identified were to be placed in the "least restrictive environment" (LRE), which is that placement most like the regular classroom that meets the need of or is appropriate to that child.

Placement, which is to be a team decision, is part of the Individual Education Plan (IEP) that the law mandates for each child. The IEP contains educational components to enhance the learning of the child as well as a prescription for special related services, if any, that should be provided to the student. Related services include but are not limited to speech therapy, occupational therapy, and physical therapy.

In 1990, Individuals with Disabilities Education Act (IDEA) was passed. IDEA amended and added to the law and regulations contained in P.L. 94-142. "IDEA added autism and traumatic brain injury as specific categories, and provided for the students with attention deficit disorder" (Podemski, Marsh, Smith, & Price 1995, p. 16). With the advent of special education legislation came the special education teacher. The special education teacher is a certified teacher specially trained to address the needs of learning disabled or mentally retarded students. Some such teachers also have training in addressing the needs of medically fragile or autistic children or children with other anomalies. The role of the special education teacher, under these laws, is to provide for the needs of the student, to assist in the development of the IEP, and to provide information for "regular" classroom teachers concerning modifications that must be made to ensure the education of the student when he or she is in the regular setting or classroom. The concept of "mainstreaming" was and is a component of these special education laws.

MAINSTREAMING

Mainstreaming means that the student is placed in the regular classroom as much as is possible and appropriate for that child. However, when special services are provided, children are "pulled out" of that regular classroom and taken to the services. No matter the degree of mainstreaming, the law contemplates that the regular teacher will be assisted by the special education teacher, who helps the regular teacher modify curriculum and instruction to maximally enhance the student's learning opportunities.

Generally, since 1975, those students who were mainstreamed into the regular classroom were there only for a limited period of time, which usually did not include time in the core classes such as math, English, social studies, or science, unless those students received indirect services. *Indirect services* means that the student's usual placement is in the regular classroom and that the special education teacher acts only as a resource to the regular teacher. Usually, students who receive indirect services reflect minimal disability and are able to function quite well in most classroom settings.

It is possible, and in many cases has been the practice, that since little monitoring is done within the regular classroom to ensure that appropriate modifications have been made for special education students, few modifications are made. This is true as well within the context of indirect services. Absent principal knowledge and appropriate monitoring/assessment, it is easy to understand, therefore, why many or most regular classroom teachers are not familiar with special education procedures at this time.

Such lack of familiarity translates into a high level of concern when those same teachers are faced with the possibility of including students with discernible disabilities in the classes they teach. Some special education teachers too are nonplussed by the possibility of inclusion, for they are concerned that it may portend a diminution of their role with special education students. Inclusion implies that students are placed in the regular classroom to the greatest possible degree and that services are brought to the student within the context of that classroom.

Whereas students were brought to the services under the initial conception of special education, this is no longer the case with included students. Special education teachers become co-teachers with regular teachers in this model. They are not only resources but also respected teaching colleagues. While regular classroom teachers may welcome such a change, the thought of having medically fragile, autistic, or mentally impaired students in their classes concerns many teachers greatly.

PROFESSIONAL CONCERNS

In the first place, many regular teachers have only had one or two higher education classes relative to the teaching of special education students. Most regular classroom teachers have taught according to their own styles, rather than those of the students, and it is the students who have had to accommodate over the years. The teaching of special education students demands the development of a new and expanded repertoire of skills for these teachers. Arguably, these skills should have been developed in the teaching of all students. They include knowledge of learning styles, modalities, and brain dominance and their impact on student learning.

Additionally, placement of special education students in the classroom requires in some cases that aides accompany those students and that accommodations for medical services be made. For teachers who are not familiar with such services, the use of communication boards, stands to hold students erect, feeding tubes, and other equipment is both daunting and threatening. For many teachers who are used to operating as solo practitioners within the classroom, the thought of having another adult present for significant periods of time is daunting as well. There is a natural insecurity that may emerge when and if a teacher believes that he or she is being critically evaluated by another educator.

CENTRAL OFFICE AND INCLUSION

The role of central office administration in light of inclusion, and indeed throughout the history of special education in schools, has been crucial to its success for teachers and students alike. All central administrators, from the superintendent to the business manager, must understand the implications and requirements of special education. The law is specific. Such services must be provided, and funds allocated must be appropriately spent to support special education students. Additionally, recent case law has supported the inclusion of students in regular classes by team decision and sometimes at the request of the parent. Among the cases that address the issue are *Oberti v. Bd. of Education of Borough of Clementon School District*, 995 F.2d 1204 (3rd Cir. 1993), *Sacramento City Unified School District v. Rachel H.*, 14 F.3d 1398 (9th Cir. 1994), and *Daniel R. R. v. State Bd. of Educ.*, 874 F.2d 1036 (5th Cir. 1989). As inclusion represents a fairly new area of case law, new cases and decisions will doubtless be forthcoming. Suffice it to say, however, that the more involved the disability of the child, the more reluctance the regular classroom teacher will generally evidence. Central office administrators, particularly those who are not special educators by training, have a crucial role in providing understanding, support, and training to regular and special education teachers alike in order to facilitate the transition to inclusive classrooms.

The message is particularly strong for parents, students, board members, and teachers if central office administrators, including the superintendent, are knowledgeable with regard to changes and provide support necessary to facilitate them. The message is simply that this is an important component of education, one that all educators are expected to support and with which all educators are expected to be involved in light of their specific responsibilities and roles. This belief coupled with collaborative teaming to achieve instructional and curricular goals for all students is a hallmark of inclusion (Villa & Thousand, 1995), but in a larger sense, it is simply good educational practice.

ADA AND SECTION 504

Teachers, patrons, and administrators often confuse the parameters of the Americans with Disabilities Act (ADA) and Section 504 with special education. The confusion, though unfortunate, is somewhat understandable for individuals who have not read the law or who do not regularly work with the law. However, it is not reasonable for anyone in school administration to fail to understand these two laws. Each of these laws is applicable to public schools but in different ways. Each carries with it accountability for administrators who fail to ensure proper application of the law.

The Americans with Disabilities Act of 1990 (Public Law 101-336), guarantees equal opportunities for individuals with disabilities by means of reasonable accommodation. The guarantee extends to public accommodations, transportation, and employment for individuals with disabilities. ADA is applicable to any institution that employs fifteen or more employees in both the public and private sectors. Certainly most school districts employ this number of individuals.

ADA provides that no employer shall discriminate against a qualified individual because of the disability of that individual. The prohibition extends to the entire hiring process, from application to promotion and even to discharge from the position should that eventuate. The assumption of the law is that such a disability impacts one or more life activities and that the individual is qualified to perform the job. There is no implication that a person must be hired solely because he or she has a disability regardless of qualifications.

Since ADA relates to employees, it also relates to the pre-employment process and the parameters within which information may be sought from applicants with disabilities. The law provides for specific limitations as to the questions that may be asked even within the interview process. Consequently, it is important not only that the administrative staff be aware of these legal guidelines but also that such information be provided through staff development to any individual at a school or departmental site within the district who may be responsible for interviewing individuals in the employment process.

The Rehabilitation Act of 1973, Section 504, speaks to the fact that "no otherwise qualified individual shall be excluded from participation in a program receiving federal financial assistance solely by reason of his handicap" (Imber & Van Geel, 1993, p. 508).

The phrase *otherwise qualified* implies that the individual is qualified to hold the position and to meet all employment requirements regardless of the disability and that he or she is not precluded from participation in an activity or program solely on the basis of the handicapping condition (Alexander & Alexander, 1995). Section 504 has implications not only for the students and teachers within our schools but also for visitors on the campus.

"Reasonable accommodation" implies exactly what it says. Reasonable accommodations are those that are feasible, both from a physical and a cost perspective, to meet the needs of the individual with disabilities. For example, although it is not necessary for a school or district to employ a hearing interpreter full-time absent the need for such an individual to work with students based on their IEPs, it is reasonable to expect one to be available when a parent with a hearing impairment comes to attend a school-initiated conference.

Section 504 relates to the need for public schools to make reasonable accommodation not only for employees but also for invitees who may be on campus, namely the parents of students who may come to school to participate in conferences, to attend performances, to be involved in or for other school-related activities. Of course, Section 504 has implications also for student participation in athletics and other school-sponsored activities.

Limitations with regard to the "reasonable accommodation" expectation are that the district does not have to incur unreasonable costs or suffer undue hardship to provide accommodation. Neither is the district called upon to make precisely the accommodation requested if in fact an alternative would provide the accommodation needed.

It is important that central office administrators, principals, and teachers understand the requirements of Section 504 and the legal meanings of the key terms in the Act. It is conceivable that not only would accommodation be necessary in regard to changes in the physical plant of a school—for example, widening door frames to accommodate a wheelchair or providing a chairlift on stairs to allow a student access to a second floor—but also in instructional accommodations within the classroom. Often teachers and principals do not focus on these changes since students who are "covered" by Section 504 may not be identified as special education students.

Teachers may need to provide large print; to seat a student in a particular area of the classroom to facilitate hearing or visual problems; to ensure that a special desk is provided; or to test a particular student orally. These are but a few of the accommodations that may be required and which teachers must work to provide within a classroom to assist students with handicapping conditions. In conjunction with appropriate central office staff, the principal, and the guidance counselor, such accommodations can be made with a minimum of disruption of the class and without major effort on the part of the teacher.

THE GIFTED STUDENT

Under the usual designation, "gifted and talented students" are students of great ability in a particular subject matter who show not only skill and mastery of material but also creativity. These above-average learning abilities and intelligence have been "traditionally defined and identified using intelligence quotient scores (IQ scores)." (Smith, Polloway, Patton, & Dowdy, 1995, p. 11). Currently, educators define giftedness as above-average abilities in the various areas of multiple intelligence as delimited by Howard Gardner (1983). These are logical-mathematical, verbal-linguistic, musical-rhythmic, visual-spatial, bodily-kinesthetic, interpersonal, and intrapersonal. Recent research might lead educators to include emotional intelligence as well (Goleman, 1995). Emotional intelligence includes such skills as the ability to motivate oneself, persistence, and self-control. All of these are basic to learning and to achievement.

Some educators are confused by gifted students, particularly by those who evidence negative behaviors and, in some cases, become behavior problems within the classroom. Principals too may be challenged by students whose abilities surpass the norm. Often these students appear to be rebellious when in fact they are not appropriately challenged within the classroom and therefore allow their creativity to lead them to challenge rules and disrupt the learning environment. Gifted students require opportunities to work with adult mentors and with a specialized, challenging curriculum that is problem-based (Lewis, 1996).

The role of the principal and of the central office administrator with reference to the gifted student is not unlike that role in relation to all other students. A prerequisite to working effectively with all students is knowledge of the program, the curriculum, and the students themselves. It behooves all administrators to know the characteristics of giftedness and to be conversant with key terminology and strategies teachers can use to benefit such students.

Administrators cannot be of assistance to teachers unless the teachers and administrators possess a common knowledge base. Additionally, administrators and teachers cannot collaborate without a common educational language. Finally, for the benefit and achievement of students, all who work with them must work as a team. Team building is crucial to strategic planning, effective collaboration, and enhanced opportunities for student learning. Team building is basic to synergy and success. As teachers and schools deal with increasing classroom diversity, collaboration among educators can be not only a support but also a source of ideas and strategies for teachers and administrators alike.

COMPENSATORY EDUCATION

The changes in federal funding that are currently affecting schools are born of the need to balance the federal budget and lower the national debt. These changes in funding have had implications for many educational programs. For example, the criteria for student and school district participation in Title I programs and consequent state changes in distribution of compensatory education moneys have both encouraged school districts to rethink their programmatic approaches to assisting students who are deficit in reading and mathematics. The new iteration of Title I places the incubus on the back of each individual district. The district must develop an individual plan for the remediation of students who have scored in the lowest quartile(s) on the district-administered standardized test.

The administrative choice is to develop the plan at central office; however, if site-based management is the focus in a school district, then the plan should be developed and implemented at the school site level with appropriate central office suggestions and assistance. This is evidence of transformational leadership not transactional leadership.

Sergiovanni (1990) defines transactional leadership as the leadership of bartering and building. This is a leadership in which "leaders and followers exchange needs and services in order to accomplish independent objectives" (p. 31). Transformative leadership, on the other hand, is in evidence in that situation in which leaders and followers "are united in pursuit of higher level goals that are common to both" (p. 31). Those goals are focused on student achievement and instructional improvement to facilitate that achievement. This is the leadership of bonding and banking, according to Sergiovanni.

VOCATIONAL EDUCATION

Vocational education students have historically been drawn from several groups of students: students who knew that they would not be going on to college; students who were consigned to vocational courses because counselors or teachers thought they could not succeed in some regular education classes; and students mandated by state or school district requirements to complete a credit in vocational education.

While "Tech Prep," which has been the vocational catchphrase in the past few years, was ostensibly adopted to cause educators and students to reconsider reasons for involvement in vocational education, in many districts, little or no change in past practice is in evidence. The Tech Prep movement is linked to a resurrection of the practice of apprenticeship in both manufacturing and service industries.

Previously, vocational offerings provided isolated skills such as drafting, carpentry, or home economics. The move to Tech Prep and apprenticeship is focused upon provision of related skills within a framework of basic curriculum, including math, English, and science, which provide a full education to the student as well as a specialization in a vocational area. School-to-work linkages provide not only a realistic hope for future employment for students but also may serve to reduce the dropout rate. However, schools and districts must be proactive in efforts to encourage local businesses and unions to consider and initiate apprenticeship programs.

Apprenticeship programs are a concomitant of and the culmination of such school-based programs as Tech Prep. Initiation of additional apprenticeship programs can only be accomplished with efforts on the part of the superintendent and other visible and credible central office administrators coordinating with principals and teachers and working with the local businesses, civic clubs, and chambers of commerce. Incentives offered to businesses and actual student-based proof of the readiness of students to enter into apprenticeship agreements upon the completion of high school are among the strongest bases for convincing the private sector that such initiatives are worthwhile (Blythe, 1991).

In this effort, the superintendent and central office administrators become the voice of teachers, the major supporters of school efforts, and communicators with the public, particularly with those who operate businesses in the community. In a sense, this is both a collaborative and a crusading role. Once the vision is developed and the district/schools begin to develop objectives and strategies to reach for that vision, the superintendent and his or her staff must share and sell the vision to the other stakeholders in the community. They should be able to demonstrate the linkage between this vision and the broader community vision of adequately educating all students for productive citizenship.

HOMELESS AND MIGRANT STUDENTS

The law demands that migrant students be provided an education in the district in which they currently reside. While the Supreme Court has upheld residency requirements as constitutional in the case of *Martinez v. Bynum* (1983), that precise decision is a "potential obstacle to the education of . . . homeless children" (Imber & Van Geel, 1993, p. 46). This is also true of migrant children. Case law, too, upholds the premise that regardless of a student's citizenship status, he or she is entitled to an education under the Fourteenth Amendment.

The increasing numbers of homeless children and, in some sections of the country, children of migrants has placed financial pressure on school districts. There are several associated problems that must be addressed. These include, but are not limited to, space concerns, the hiring of additional teachers in order to maintain reasonable class sizes, and the employment of English as a second language (ESL) teachers.

Planning, both educational and fiscal, is necessary to address the needs of these students and to prepare teachers to address their educational needs. Other supports may need to be provided by way of staff development for teachers, incentives to encourage teachers and principals to keep current with professional readings relative to these students, and modeling of such behaviors by the central office administrators, including the superintendent.

STUDENTS WITH HEALTH CARE ISSUES

Students with health care issues may be covered by Section 504. Those who are ill but who do not have a disability that falls within Section 504 parameters still require attention in order to be successful within the school. Such attention may take the form of teacher awareness, records kept with the school nurse, and/or provision for modifications in class presentation and material to assist the student with learning. Additionally, it will be the responsibility of the superintendent and his or her staff to develop and update policy with regard to student illness and communicable disease. Appropriate policies and procedures developed to accompany them can be of great assistance to site principals and teachers in their day-to-day interactions with students.

In cases in which regulations must be accompanied by training or materials and supplies, such as latex gloves or disinfectants, it is the responsibility of the central administration to provide such items to principals and their staffs. Likewise, it is the responsibility of the central office staff to ensure that policies and procedures comply with relevant law, which includes both case law and state codes. These laws include not only those which relate to supervision and treatment of these students but also to the privacy rights of students and their records. Finally, it is the responsibility of the central office—the superintendent as well as line and staff personnel—to ensure that all stakeholders are adequately informed in a timely fashion as to both policy and applicable procedures. These stakeholders include the board, school staffs, and patrons.

STUDENTS IN NEED OF DISCIPLINARY INTERVENTION AND OTHER "AT RISK" STUDENTS

The superintendent and his or her staff has a duty to work with building principals and with teachers to ensure that learning is not disrupted by students who are discipline problems. Likewise, it is the responsibility of the superintendent to work to provide a safe environment conducive to learning for both teachers and students. These duties would include the development of a coherent disciplinary policy that is shared with students, patrons, and the public. Appropriate penalties for misbehavior should be implemented. Such penalties must comport with the law and should be such that they result in improved behavior but tend not to exclude students from school unless absolutely necessary. Students who are behind in their work often fail to catch up and may become dropouts. Exclusion from school for lengthy periods of time may exacerbate these problems.

Simultaneously, teachers should be trained with regard to relevant disciplinary policy and related legal parameters. The superintendent in a small district will probably have to take this responsibility on himself or herself or make provisions for it to be assumed by staff. Superintendents in larger districts may have staff designated to identify professional development needs. Whatever is the case, the superintendent must set the expectation that such training will be provided and that teachers will act in concert with policy and the law. The result of failure to address such concerns is lost time in the form of time spent in disciplinary hearings or in court and also lost time in classrooms as teachers try nonproductively to address disciplinary issues.

In some districts, alternative education has been used to address the learning and behavioral needs of students who are frequent and serious offenders. Such interventions include night school using regular school sites, the establishment of time out of the school or alternative classrooms within the school itself, or the establishment of a separate alternative school. Any of these can work if the students are appropriately monitored and taught and their learning needs are met. Such interventions will only be successful, however, if they are based in solid understandings with regard to appropriate behavioral interventions, the learning styles and needs of the individual students, and instruction by teachers who are effective in working with at-risk youth.

Most important, such interventions will not work unless and until the superintendent has and shares a vision concerning mediation for at-risk students with all of the staff and teachers. They will not work until all are committed to work together to intervene with and assist these students to be successful. They will not work until all are productively engaged in planning for and designing alternative programs for students. Such collaboration recognizes teacher skills, creates ownership in and commitment to the program, and greatly enhances the probability of success.

CHANGES IN ADMINISTRATIVE ROLE

Changes that must accompany administration of programs for special needs students include a broadened knowledge base on the part of all staff, from superintendent to preschool teacher. There must also be a shared vision, a collaborative development of goals and strategies, and a maximum utilization of teacher skills for design and implementation. Imposed changes seldom work, and they never last beyond the tenure of the superintendent and the board. Of course, it is crucial that the school board be knowledgeable of, supportive of, and committed to all programs within the district.

Herein lies a major role and responsiblity of the superintendent, for it is he or she who must educate, support, cajole, and train the board concerning the needs that exist and the value of these programs for addressing them. The superintendent must make the board cognizant of the legal implications of their actions and remind them of legal requirements that must be met. It is also the responsibility of the superintendent to constantly assess, or provide for assessment of, programs and their impact so that the board may make decisions that benefit students and teachers predicated on reliable data and sound information.

REFERENCES

Alexander, K. & Alexander, M. D. (1995). *The law of schools, students and teachers.* St. Paul, MN: West Publishing Co.

Blythe, J. R. (December 1991). Preventing school dropout. *The Education Digest.* pp. 32–38.

Daniel R. R. v. State Bd. of Educ., 874 F.2d 1036 (5th Cir. 1989).

Gardner, H. (1983). *Frames of mind: The theory of multiple intelligences.* NY: Basic Books.

Goleman, D. (1995). *Emotional intelligence: Why it can matter more than IQ.* NY: Bantam Books.

Imber, M. & Van Geel, T. (1993) *Education law.* NY: McGraw-Hill.

Lewis, B. A. (1996) Serving others hooks gifted students on learning. *Educational Leadership* 53(5):70–74.

Martinez v. Bynum, 461 U.S. 321(1983).

Oberti v. Bd. of Education of Borough of Clementon School District, 995 F.2d 1204 (3rd Cir. 1993)

Podemski, R. S., Marsh, G. E. , Smith, T. E. C., & Price, B. J. (1995). *Comprehensive administration of special education.* Englewood Cliffs, NJ: Merrill.

Sergiovanni, T. J. (1990). *Value-added leadership.* New York: Harrcourt, Brace, Jovanovich.

Smith, T. C. C., Polloway, E. A., Patton, J. R., and Dowdy, C. A. (1995). *Teaching children in inclusive settings,* Needham Heights, MA: Allyn & Bacon.

Villa, R.A. & Thousand, J.S. (eds.) (1995). *Creating an inclusive school.* Alexandria, VA: ASCD.

Sacramento City Unified School District v. Rachel H., 14 F.3d 1398 (9th Cir. 1994).

CHAPTER 9

Planning and Evaluation from a Central Office–School Partnership Perspective

The daily operations of school districts can have no real focus without a planning process. Results of decisions and programs will have little utility absent systematic, meaningful evaluation. Process and product are of importance at the inception of any idea or decision and are crucial when testing the effects of that idea or decision. Assessment and planning do not just happen, however.

FROM VISION TO PLAN

WHEN embarking on a trip, it is generally good practice to secure a map, to plan the days' journeys, and to secure lodging for the night both en route and at the destination, wherever that may be. It is also helpful to know the destination because such knowledge certainly aids in the process of packing. The operations of a school district, particularly in the current milieu, replete as it is with calls for change, are not unlike a journey.

First and foremost, the leadership of the district must possess and share a vision. The board and superintendent may generate the vision, but without the sharing of that vision with others, little progress toward its realization will be made. Generally, the vision is viewed as the apex, the tip of an isosceles triangle that focuses the district. Indeed, vision provides focus, but in a real sense, the vision is also the base from which all other educational activities emanate. Vision, when shared and discussed, naturally leads to a mission statement. The vision is the finished product, the image of what is to evolve from the educational process to benefit students and society. The mission statement is more specific or tangible than the vision. A mission statement may be understood even by those who haven't quite captured the vision. It enables these individuals to begin the process of visualizing what can be.

From the mission statement emanates the goals, objectives, and strategies which the district and each component of the district will employ to achieve the mission and reach toward the vision. Goals and objectives are even more specific. For example, separate goals may be written to address each component of the mission statement. Objectives reflect goals but differ in that they clearly tell the district employees and customers what will be different, by when, and how that change will be measured.

PLANNING LEVELS

Key to the development of goals, objectives, and strategies is team building. Each client or stakeholder involved in the district must be aware of and committed to both vision and process. Awareness and commitment must be developed at the Mega, Macro, and Micro levels (Kaufman, 1992). The Mega level generally denotes the community in which the school system exists and operates. The Macro level is the district itself, and the Micro level is the schools. At the school planning level, one might think of the Mega level as the district and/or the community of individuals whose children attend that particular school, while the Macro level would be the entire school, and the Micro level, the individual classroom. If the entire population of a level cannot be involved, then at least a representative sample must be in order to ensure commitment and support for the plans and decisions that must be made to reach the district vision.

At this juncture, it may be well to define our terms by means of examples. *Vision* denotes the broad picture of where the district will be at a certain time. For example, a vision might be that the *Freedom District will be one in which all students master the knowledge base and citizenship skills*. From the vision is drawn a mission statement; for example: *Students in the Freedom District will be academically competent, active, and knowledgeable citizens able to function effectively in a changing world*. Goals are more specific. Goals to accompany the previously stated mission statement might be:

- to teach and test students for mastery in all subjects
- to instruct students in the competencies necessary to make sound judgments and to effectively exercise their citizenship rights and responsibilities.

- to develop and implement a curriculum that encompasses appropriate knowledge bases and citizenship competencies for students.
- to provide an environment/climate in the school that is supportive of and conducive of teaching and learning

Objectives, as previously noted, delineate what will be different, in what time period it will be different, and in what manner it will be measured. For example, goal #1 may be accompanied by an objective that reads:

- All students in the Freedom District will pass the state-mandated competency examination at the 75th percentile or above during each student's senior year beginning with the class of 2000 A.D.

From the stated objective, strategies are developed, responsibility is assigned, and timelines are established. Formatting these will allow a district administration, as well as its teachers, patrons, and students, the opportunity to assess progress in an orderly manner and to provide resources appropriately to support efforts to reach the goal or goals.

TOOLS FOR PLANNING

In the development and implementation of strategies to meet goals, Kurt Lewin's (1947) force field analysis may be a helpful tool. Teams of stakeholders, including students, may meet to discuss and prepare the force field analysis that allows participants to identify restraining forces and the driving forces relative to goal achievement. Restraining forces may be weaknesses in staffing, skills, support, or programs that could negatively impact efforts at achieving goals. Restraining forces may also be represented by threats, real or perceived, which the schools or district face. For example, strong opposition to a needed millage that would enable the district to implement a new program is a threat.

Driving forces may be strengths that individuals or programs represent that would substantially assist the change effort or enhance goal focus. Other driving forces are opportunities that present themselves or are identified. For example, a district that normally could not afford to bring in a nationally known educator to train staff may ascertain that the individual will be in a neighboring city and could come to the district for a reduced rate because travel expenses would not be a factor. Certainly this would provide an opportunity to acquire staff or public training that otherwise might not be available.

After identification of driving and restraining forces, the focus of objectives that support the goals is enhanced by heightened awareness of those advantages the district has and those situations that could negatively impact the effort to achieve a goal. Such awareness allows the opportunity for systematic planning rather than reactive behaviors on the part of central office and other administrators. It is important that all interested parties be engaged in the brainstorming process by which driving and restraining forces are identified, since each constituency will have knowledge and experience that others might not possess.

Additionally, collaboration on and identification of perceived driving and restraining forces will engage stakeholders and give them ownership in the process of working to achieve goals and objectives. It will enable all partners in the educational enterprise to develop a common language and common concerns. Finally, collaboration ensures that the beliefs and values of the stakeholders are factored into the planning process.

ROLE OF CENTRAL OFFICE ADMINISTRATORS

Central office administrators and principals should be trained to facilitate these processes to ensure smooth functioning and their ultimate success. Since it is crucial that stakeholders in an organization be able to communicate with each other in a "thorough, open, and accurate fashion" (Greenberg, 1996), central office administrators, particularly the superintendent, must model open communication, true brainstorming without criticism of individuals, and discussion without the use of "educationese." Educators are as adept at jargon as any other profession, and its use can be as negatively received by the layman as such language is in other endeavors such as law and medicine.

A crucial role for the facilitator in a goal setting process is that of explaining the terminology and parameters to all participants prior to engaging in the actual planning activity. (Even school board members may require some practice in the process from time to time in order to hone their individual skills.) It is the responsibility of the central office staff, under the leadership of the superintendent, to ensure that all planning participants understand the process and are familiar with terminology and expectations. In other words, all participants must have the total information they need in order to be productive participants in this crucial activity.

In a sense, central office administrators must also become gatekeepers. That is to say that once ground rules are set, the superintendent and his or her staff must ensure that the rules remain in effect, absent a decision by all planning participants to change these rules. None of these central office roles is top-down, and each represents a collegial role for the central office administrator. Each squarely places that administrator in a partnership position vis-à-vis others in the planning process. In no case does this diminish either the power or authority of the administrator; rather, it allows that administrator to operate based on expert rather than positional or coercive power and on functional and informal authority rather than only traditional or legal authority (Hoy & Miskel, 1996). The facilitative postures assumed by the central administration also serve to empower school site administrators to emulate the planning process at their own schools and with their own patrons and staffs. These behaviors likewise provide a model that school principals may follow in order to foster team decision making and to foster collaboration among all stakeholders in the individual school's success.

ACTION RESEARCH

An important advantage of an orderly planning process is that school site and district administrators may use the goal-setting process and those data that support it as baseline information in action research. Action research involves assessing the plan of action and its effectiveness once implemented. The process consists of gathering appropriate data comparisons at identified points in the implementation process to ascertain whether the objective is being achieved. If so, the process continues. If not, the plans must be reassessed and modified in order to enhance the prospect of goal achievement. If, for example, a teacher-made test or a standardized pre-test indicates that students are not mastering the knowledge base required, then the planning and implementing of modifications in curriculum and delivery of instruction take place as a normal part of the process.

EVALUATION/ASSESSMENT

No planning process is complete without appropriate assessment of progress. To paraphrase an old saying, if you don't know where you are going, then anyplace you arrive will do. In education, we do not have the luxury of arriving just anyplace in today's international society. It is probable that we never did, although we may have thought this was the case during the time when the United States had a positive balance of trade and our schools were not negatively compared to those of other industrialized countries.

Assessment of progress must be both formative and summative. Formative assessment is assessment of a process while it is ongoing. Summative assessment is assessment of the product and of the process after its completion. In any planning rubric, there are points at which participants attempt to gain some sense of whether or not they are traveling in the right direction. On a journey, it is not uncommon for an automobile traveler to consult a map or for an airline traveler to check the flight schedule at an airport several times to ensure that the intended destination will be reached in a timely manner. So it is with an effective planning process.

There are en route checkpoints built into the agenda, points at which progress toward reaching the objectives and the broader goal is assessed. These are natural reporting points at which a superintendent, board members, principals, and other key players meet with and report to all constituents. These are points at which necessary modifications are made in timelines, resources, and responsibilities, and new strategies may be put into action. Formative evaluation provides a monitoring function in the process of goal achievement. Since change is achieved only by means of a difficult and often slow process, evaluation can provide both encouragement and information for those persons engaged in modifying practice and performance or results.

A positive result of formative evaluation, or monitoring, is that it will tend to lessen the apprehension that those who will be held accountable for results, generally teachers, students, and site administrators, may feel relative to the final evaluation of goal achievement. Monitoring in process can encourage individuals to do their best while simultaneously reducing tension (Greenberg, 1996) and apprehension to a productive level. (Tension experienced at an appropriate level may improve output, while tension that is too severe or lacking in impact will tend to negatively impact production and its attendant quality.)

Evaluation is not a process in which the intent is to catch people failing at their work. Rather, evaluation is ideally a practice by which the work of individuals and the impact of programs can be improved. It is crucial that the superintendent and central office administrators model this belief in their behaviors relative to evaluation. Wissler and Ortiz (1988) point this out when they write of a superintendent who endeavored to teach his central office staff "to become a service, not a command structure" (p. 151).

This behavior creates the type of organization in which people are empowered, in which individuals communicate openly, and in which innovative work can be done. Evaluation in such an organization is not viewed as punitive, but rather it is seen as productive of enhanced focus, additional support for goal achievement, and an opportunity to experiment based on solid data and to share ideas and proven models for success. Such a model for evaluation builds collegiality and collaboration rather than inspiring conflictual competition. It creates a climate in schools and districts that is energizing rather than debilitating. In such a climate parents, teachers, students, administrators, and community members take ownership of the schools and focus on doing all that is necessary to ensure success and an appropriate education for every student.

PROCESS STEPS

Steps in this process which central office personnel might follow and which will facilitate a climate of empowerment, innovation, and investment are:

- frequent school site visits that focus on collaboration and open communication rather than directives for change
- meetings with principals, teachers, students, and patrons that focus on sharing of ideas and valid information relative to district goals and objectives
- opportunities for patrons and community members to be in the schools and to serve in meaningful capacities in planning and assessment processes
- a commitment to use the ideas of others that are generated through involvement, collaboration and committee service
- a "no surprise" rule that is understood, adopted, and implemented.

A "no surprise" rule implies that in the case of both negative and positive feedback, ample discussion, and mutual access to and consideration of data are the rule. Additionally, suggestions for change and improvement will be generated predicated on an awareness of the readiness level of the individual being assessed or on accurate information relative to the program being evaluated. On such parameters the climate and conditions necessary for change must be based. It is the fair and consistent implementation of such parameters as well as respect for the expertise each stakeholder brings to the enterprise that will be the ultimate arbiters of both the planning and evaluation processes in this age of change in educational priority and expectations.

The role of the central office administrator is to recognize the need for and to facilitate understanding and implementation of planning and evaluation. This role is the crucial component in the effort to ensure that the vision of educational and personal excellence can be reached by each student in the care of the school or district and by each staff member in his or her role relative to that educational process.

REFERENCES

Greenberg, J. (1996). *Managing behavior in organizations.* Upper Saddle River, NJ: Prentice Hall.

Hoy, W. K. & Miskel, C. G. (1996). *Educational administration: Theory, research, and practice* (5th ed.). NY: McGraw-Hill.

Kaufman, R. (1992). *Mapping educational success.* Newbury Park, CA: Corwin Press.

Lewin, K. (June, 1947). "Frontiers in group dynamics: Concepts, method, and reality in social science." *Human Relations,* 1(1): 5–41.

Wissler, D. F & Ortiz, F. I. (1988). *The superintendent's leadership in school reform.* NY: The Falmer Press.

CHAPTER 10

Central Office Business Functions

Central office business functions should support the educational process by ensuring the existence of a climate conducive to learning and maximizing cost-benefit efficiency within the district.

ALTHOUGH the business side of school district operations is generally unnoticed in the day-to-day educational process, its smooth and efficient functioning is basic to and crucial for the continuation of the educational process in schools. Unfortunately, it is often only when there is a fiscal difficulty in a school system or a major problem in transportation of students or a need for building repair that financial and business functions receive adequate attention from the public and school personnel. At that point, the work of the fiscal officer, superintendent, or principal is diverted from instructional support to troubleshooting. Although troobleshooting is part of the job, finance, like all other aspects of the educational enterprise, requires planning and should be such a smoothly functioning aspect of operations that it is not a source of concern on a daily basis for anyone other than those charged with financial management.

In a sense, this means that the purview of the principal as it relates to finances will be limited. This is not surprising as the day-to-day business functions are not located at schools, and the manager of those functions, except in the situation of a very small district, is more knowledgeable about the business side of education than any other administrator. Often it is true also that no other administrator really cares to know more about school business functions than is absolutely necessary. After all, educators are trained to address instruction, curriculum, and discipline primarily.

In fact, many higher education institutions that offer courses for certification and advanced degrees in school administration do not require their students to take a course in school finance. Generally, that course is offered only to individuals who aspire to be superintendents or school district business managers. This may be an unwise practice, particularly in light of the move toward site based management. If a school district is contemplating or engaged in a move toward site-based management, it is essential that all administrators, including building principals, have a thorough understanding of finances, financial management, and the purchasing process.

The school board members too should be given some training relative to the various funds a school district must manage, general operating budget (usually called maintenance and operations), capital outlay, and debt service. Additionally, board members need to possess at least a rudimentary understanding of the sources of the revenue the district receives. The terminology with which all administrators and board members should have some familiarity includes but is not limited to:

- restricted and unrestricted funds (funds that may be spent for specified uses versus funds that may be spent for any legitimate educational use)
- fixed and variable costs: costs that once set during a year will not change—for example, teachers salaries—versus costs that change according to economic trends—for example, the cost of fuel for buses
- direct and indirect costs: costs that accrue directly to a school or district office versus those that are averaged over the district or several schools. Teachers in a building are a direct cost, while the superintendent is an indirect cost to the individual school.
- average daily membership and average daily enrollment: the former is the average number of days students are in class, while the latter relates to the average number of days students were carried on the roll, without reference to absences.
- encumbrances: moneys committed and therefore no longer available for use.
- per-pupil expenditures: an average figure derived from all costs directly associated with the school or an average derived from dividing all district costs by the total number of students enrolled in the entire district.

A sound knowledge of the state funding formula and state law with regard to millages, teacher salary parameters, per-pupil expenditure minimums (if any), and other legal requirements must also be a part of the information that the superintendent and school district finance manager must have. Additionally, the board cannot develop good policy without a basic understanding of the financial issues and requirements that must be addressed by the district administration.

The superintendent and the school board should have a basic understanding of fiscal constraints and requirements as well as legal exigencies. It is also most helpful if principals have a similar knowledge base. These informational pieces are fundamental to good communication as well as sound financial practices at the school and district levels. Additionally, they facilitate a set of common understandings and a common language among administrators in the district. That in itself can serve to enhance efficiency, effectiveness, and equity. An objective of schools today is to provide equity (Candoli, Hack & Ray, 1992, p. 11). Equity, of course, relates to the delivery of support to all students, regardless of need. Equity means that students with greater needs will be afforded greater support.

LINKING FOR EFFICIENCY

As in any aspect of school governance and day-to-day operations, good communication is important. Communication systems should encompass all available modes of transmission: face-to-face contact, oral discussion, written memo, and the use of e-mail and administrative list serves. Unfortunately, some schools, districts, and educators are not yet conversant with technology and its many uses. Some do not have access to the latest technological hardware and software.

Some of the processes that are fundamental to an efficient and supportive business component within a school district are purchasing, warehousing, maintenance of inventory, the use of technology to create work orders, and access to daily balances in each school account. In fact, it is not uncommon for districts to use computers as well for the routing of buses rather than using human time and energy for the purpose of establishing bus stops and assigning students to buses.

Arguably, software is expensive and updating hardware is an ongoing and somewhat onerous task. However, even small districts may pool resources to purchase or access hardware and software that would be useful for facilitating business functions and daily operations.

In some states (for example, Arkansas), provisions have been made to put into place a statewide network for purposes of communications among schools and within districts. Of course, the schools must purchase the hardware and take care of the wiring. A state menu for schools is available that allows schools to use e-mail and to develop district or school home pages. Likewise, there is a state financial spreadsheet in the system that allows school district fiscal officers and their designees to follow a standard format using technology and to file reports and other pertinent fiscal and budgetary information directly with the state department and the office of finance and administration without having to hand enter (type) data on standardized print forms as has been done in the past.

The use of technology can serve also to facilitate the filing of state reports in other areas, such as free and reduced-cost lunch information, that the state monitors on behalf of the federal government. Accreditation reports may also be filed with the state department via the list serve or e-mail used by the state. In each case, the work of the state is reduced and the data collected by the district may be efficiently stored and easily retrieved by state and district alike.

TECHNOLOGY FOR CURRICULAR EFFICIENCY

The curricular supports that are so often present in a school district may be either an onerous source of expenditures or a well-considered, fairly costly, and instructionally beneficial. The instructional benefit of well-chosen software, videos, and recommended texts cannot be denied if the material and concepts addressed in these are aligned with the district curriculum. However, it is true that absent such alignment, expenditures on "interesting" materials that appeal to teachers may not be optimal in light of the budgetary restrictions districts face. In fact, most districts have only 20–30% of their current revenue available for expenditure in the general (maintenance and operations) fund after certified salaries and fringe benefits are paid. The remaining revenue must be expended on noncertified staff salaries, general maintenance and repair costs, texts, supplies, and other materials necessary to support instruction. There are clearly few dollars available for use in the purchase of supplemental curricular materials.

Consequently, it is necessary for all expenditures to be made wisely. Additionally, the staff—teachers, administrators, and aides—must maximize the utility of all purchases. This can be done quite simply through the use of technology. "The planned instructional acquisition and use of software (and other supporting materials) might be addressed in five different ways" (Sewall, 1994, p. 44). These include assessment of needs, planned acquisition, centralized access, instructional application guidelines, and evaluation of the materials. These modes for curricular planning should be used cyclically and should definitely be employed at the time of each new textbook adoption. The central office administration, in the form of designated administrators, can easily take the lead in developing task forces to participate in these endeavors to ensure teacher, school site administrator, and public input.

Financial savings and efficiency are to be realized in terms of the use of a district list serve for the purpose of posting all available supplementary forms and information. The listing would also show where such materials and supplies are located (housed) within the district and would indicate whether or not the texts, software, and other educational items were in current use and by whom. Obviously there will be situations in which material is used so often that several copies must be purchased. Other software, videos, and supplemental texts may be used relatively infrequently and could be shared among teachers by virtue of a good scheduling process. In either situation, there is still a significant monetary savings to be realized as it will not be necessary to purchase such materials for every teacher and may not even be necessary to purchase them for each school. Centralized access, whether at an instructional resource center or through the list serve, will "facilitate teacher awareness of what is available and make it easier to locate materials." (Sewall, 1994, p. 44). Each teacher may be asked to evaluate this system and the materials used as they are used and to return the completed evaluation form to the appropriate central office personnel. Compiled evaluations become useful tools for assistance in planning future purchases.

Of course, in order to effect such a system, an initial investment in technology is necessary. Additionally, each teacher should have access to the technology and list serve and each teacher will require a certain level of technological competence in order to effectively use the system to maximize curricular support and foster fiscally sound educational decisions.

FACILITATED CURRICULAR DEVELOPMENT

The use of technology can assist with savings and the ability of the district and schools to reallocate dollars in other significant ways. For example, if technology is available to teachers and time is provided, there is software available that will allow teachers to develop programs for purposes of teaching concepts and skills within their own subject areas.

Teachers in some school districts have used software to describe, draw, or scan and animate birds for science classes. Appropriate avian songs were added to spice up the presentation. Other teachers have developed maps that modify themselves to show changes in Africa, Russia, and Asia as a means of supplementing discussion in history classes. Still other teachers have created tutorials and self-assessments for use by students as they try to master concepts in all subjects. Not only is the development of such materials satisfying to teachers and helpful to students, but it is also cost-effective. The only real cost is the teacher's time and an initial investment in a site license for computer software.

Districts or schools may choose to pay an incentive to teachers for the development and dissemination of subject matter programs and demonstrations utilizing technology. The cost of incentives is much less than the cost of purchasing materials from a vendor, particularly if those materials are software programs. Additionally, materials created by teachers for their students will tend to reflect the curriculum more accurately than will programs purchased from vendors, who tend to sell generic materials.

ENVIRONMENTAL SUPPORT

The physical facilities in which teachers work and students learn can influence the learning. Not only is it important to conduct school within a clean and orderly environment, but it is also important that the visual field, auditory background, lighting, and temperature be conducive to the learning and teaching processes. "Instructional spaces are central to any positive learning and teaching environment" (Herman, 1995, p. 10).

The work of the central office administration is, in part, to ensure that such conducive conditions exist. Although it is true that the principal must provide supervision and support at the school site by working with the custodians, the central administration in districts of all size must take the major role in supporting building cleanliness and maintenance. The model for this varies according to district size.

In a small district, custodians will generally be in the employ of the district, but any repairs, renovation, or simple construction will be contracted with community businesses. In medium-sized districts, the same process may be followed for renovation and simple construction, but general repairs are made by plant service employees hired by the district. (Such repairs may include painting, plastering, changing heat and air filters, and repairing or replacing locks.) Most large school districts have a plant services department that handles all of the discussed categories of repair and maintenance. Districts of all sizes contract with architects for building designs and with construction companies for the building of facilities, however.

One important component of effective central office administration, in light of site-based management, is the involvement of school staff and administrators in the planning process for new construction or repair and renovation at schools. The central office administrator, whether superintendent or plant services director, must coordinate construction planning and ensure the involvement of appropriate personnel. For example, no one will pay closer attention to the space needed for a counselor or nurse than the counselor or nurse. Although architects and school administrators may know the space standards established by state law and by the American Institute of Architects, those who will use space will be most conscientious in assuring compliance with standards and the meeting of needs.

Principals also have a stake in the design of new buildings and new spaces within existing buildings. It is important that building areas be manageable both from the perspective of traffic flow and in terms of visibility by teachers and administrators. A good visual area is key to the effective supervision of students. Office space must be designed in a manner conducive to the appropriate transaction of business and in a pattern where patrons and students to be counseled or disciplined will remain focused on their business in the office area.

It is strongly suggested that a method of generating work orders be in place that will save time for principals and facilitate repairs. Of course, the use of an administrative list serve will accomplish this. A format for generating work orders can be included in the district software that principals may access. Upon completion of the form, a number will be assigned to the work to be done. Plant services secretaries or the appropriate administrator can then ensure the completion of work in a timely manner and monitor that completion.

BUDGETING—DISTRICT AND SITE

As previously noted, only a small percentage of educational revenues are available for supplies, material, and equipment. Most of the school district budget is allocated to personnel costs, salaries, and fringe benefits. "Another 8 to 9 percent of total costs are allocated to fixed costs . . . over which little control can be exercised" (Candoli, Hack & Ray, 1992, p. 115). These fixed costs include utilities, insurance, and interest. The remaining dollars, generally less than 10% of available funds, are all that can be used for instructional support.

In the traditional budgeting experience, the central office administration recommends the hiring of staff to the school board upon recommendation of the principal and approval of the superintendent. Salaries, benefits, and indeed the number of positions (f.t.e.'s, or full-time equivalents) budgeted for any school site are finally determined by central office administrators, generally the business manager in consultation with the superintendent and/or assistant superintendent responsible for supervision of the particular school. These decisions are made predicated on enrollment, applicable state and contractual standards, and, at the secondary level, the student course request tallies. Of course, the principal can allocate teachers to grades and subjects and may even argue for an increase in faculty or staff positions. In general, however, those numbers are set based on the previously noted factors and budgetary constraints and are not subject to negotiation.

In a district that is in the process of reformation or that has a true site-based management system in place, principals are given a dollar allocation and may spend that money as they see fit for the purpose of providing quality instruction for students. This in no way implies that principals are not finally accountable for their decisions or that they may not be called upon to explain them, but rather that the process of budgeting and allocation of staff and materials at the school site is properly located at the school site. The role of the central administration is to provide advice and consent. However, even in a district that has fully adopted site-based management, the superintendent is ultimately accountable and must report to a school board that has the authority to fire him or her. Training and support must be provided for principals in order to facilitate their ability to effectively manage budgeting and staffing processes. Staffing and budgeting decisions may be made effectively if made close to the actual situation. Decisions will tend to be made with greater attention to detail, economy, and concern about relevant educational outcomes if they are made at the school site by the principal and his or her staff in consultation with supportive central administrators.

CENTRALIZED AND DECENTRALIZED ACTIVITY

"The advantages of centralized or of decentralized budgeting is affected greatly by the underlying view of the administrator regarding control or power" (Drake & Roe, 1994, p. 74). Of course, some components of the process will remain in the hands of central administration for purposes of efficiency and economy. Such support includes warehousing, purchasing of supplies and materials and texts, human resources support services, maintenance workers other than custodians, student transportation, centralized data processing, and intradistrict mail services.

In some districts, principals are given money to hire their own custodians, aides, and food service workers in addition to teachers. Any money that they are able to save by means of increased efficiency and individualized school site economy can be spent in any ways the principal sees fit in order to support the instructional process and student achievement. This provides an incentive to principals and their staffs and enhances school site accountability in the budgeting and expenditure processes.

In fact, in some districts, the principal's initial budgetary involvement each year is in the form of a budget he or she constructs, proposes, and defends to the superintendent. If the budget is feasible and the district has adequate resources, that principal will be allocated the requested dollars. He or she is responsible not only for good stewardship of the dollars but also for demonstrable instructional improvement as a result of the activity and personnel funded within the school by means of the budgeted amount. The empowerment inherent in such site-based management activities is apparent. It professionalizes the principalship, has the potential to engage teachers in participatory decision making, and provides an opportunity for the patrons of a school to take an active role in planning, saving, and working for their own schools. Site-based management "is basically an attempt to transform schools into communities where the appropriate people participate constructively in major decisions that affect them" (David, 1996, p. 4).

REFERENCES

Candoli, I. C., Hack, W. G., & Ray, J. R. (1992). *School business administration: A planning approach* (4th ed.). Boston: Allyn & Bacon.

David, J. L. (1996). "The who, what, and why of site-based management." *Educational Leadership.* 53(4): 4–9.

Drake, T. L. & Roe, W. H. (1994). *School business management: Supporting instructional effectiveness.* Needham Heights, MA: Allyn & Bacon.

Herman, J. J. (1995). Effective school facilities. Lancaster, PA: Technomic Publishing Co., Inc.

Sewall, A. M. (1994). "Linking learning: Managing technology for enhanced learning." *Tech Trends.* 39(6): 43–45.

CHAPTER 11

Public Relations, the Media and Selling the District

Public relations is not an area in which some central administrators choose to dabble. For others, it is the real joy of the job. No matter which is the case, public relations, particularly with and through the media, can be a major determinant of the success or failure of the superintendent, board, and district.

FEW areas of administrative practice afford the superintendent and his or her central office staff more opportunities to engage in transformational leadership than public relations. Yukl and Tracey (1992) describe transformational leadership as leading for change. This definition is in sharp contrast to the concept of transactional leadership, that is, leading for stability. Transformational leadership implies the empowerment of others. Transactional leadership focuses primarily on problem solving. Of course, the leadership styles evidence a choice in terms of leadership priorities.

The leadership and communication skills of any superintendent are often put to the test when dealing with the public and the media. Patrons often think of schools only in the context of their own school experiences as children. Those who have children in the schools may tend to believe that while their own children's schools are good, schools in general are ineffectual and unsafe for students. (Year after year, the national poll conducted by *Phi Delta Kappa* has demonstrated the truth of these statements.) Public opinion is often formed of gleanings from the media as well as word-of-mouth information regarding events and attitudes at various schools.

If a transformational leader is exemplified by the vision he or she has and shares with regard to excellence in education, then it is the communications and public relations skills the leader possesses that help to translate and share that vision with all of the publics with which a school district works. Leadership could even be defined as personal influence that assists in the achievement of goals through the communication process.

Indeed, in small and moderate-sized school districts, the superintendent is a key leader in the community and in all community decision making. In larger school districts, the superintendent may or may not enjoy such high visibility in the community. Nonetheless, his or her skill in working with press and public alike will be major determinants of the public perception of the district and consequently of the success of millage elections and schools in general.

PUBLIC RELATIONS PROGRAMS

In a joint publication by the American Association of School Administrators and the National School Boards Association (*Roles and Relationships,* 1994), the following recommendations are made relative to the development of an effective public relations program:

- policies that ensure open communications
- regular formal and informal surveys of community attitudes, opinions and needs
- involvement of community members in advisory groups in decisions that affect them
- publications that carry information, ideas, and opinions to the community
- identification and tracking of issues, trends, or conditions that could affect the ability of the school district to reach its goals

It is important that teachers and teacher associations as well as all other district employees are included among those publics with whom the central office must communicate. School site staff, indeed all staff, are potentially powerful purveyors of either positive or negative information that may serve as a major factor in the molding of public opinion. It is the teachers and students who tell the story of schools and education in the community that the members of that community will be most likely to believe.

To this end, a superintendent should have a public relations program in place that is composed of internal and external communication components. The program must provide guidelines for addressing and sharing good news, bad news, and general information in crisis situations. It is a wise school district administration that has similar plans in effect at each school and program site. Such site plans must be coordinated with and reflective of the district level communication plans and procedures.

WORKING WITH THE MEDIA

Many administrators are tempted to assume that members of the press are their friends. The fact that a few anecdotes have been exchanged or that a certain reporter has been generous in past writings does not portend continuation of that behavior in the present or future. The salary of a reporter, whether print or video, is predicated on the gathering of information for publication. This is simply the fact of the matter and in no way denigrates the value of the role played by the media. It is an understanding that educators must have however.

No comment is ever really "off the record." Consequently, administrators should not be surprised to read any comments they have made—even purportedly "off the record"—in the daily paper the next day. As comments, whether off or on the record, are the stock and trade of the press, so sound bites are the vehicle for transmission of the news employed by radio and television reporters. Administrators and school site personnel whose responsibility it is to communicate with the media would do well to remember that sound bites are selected and selective. Consequently, it is important that what is communicated is specific, focused, complete, and brief. All of these items are essential if the essence of the message is to be conveyed as intended to the community.

Additionally, if the lines of communication are clear and understood within the district, the superintendent and school site administrators can exchange information and keep each other updated as necessary on every issue to ensure such clarity in providing information to the media. Public controversy is particularly stressful for the superintendent and his or her staff, the school board, and school staffs. Although such controversy may arise from time to time over issues ranging from curriculum to methods for student discipline to the establishment of clinics at schools, good communication can reduce the stress and lessen the divisions for all concerned parties.

Such communication may be anticipatory, that is, in anticipation of a change that is to be proposed or that will take place. (Change often causes discomfort and controversy.) In an article entitled "Calming Controversy," Derrington (1993) notes that the superintendent must keep board and staff informed. She further states that "another essential group that requires full and complete information is the press. Don't wait for one of your loudest critics to call the newspaper or television station. Initiate regular conversations with key reporters" (p. 34). She also advises that comments be rehearsed and that conversation be limited to those comments using a friendly rather than a defensive tone but carefully telling the full story.

Even in calm periods of time, this is good advice and may assist superintendent and school leaders in allaying controversy before it begins. However, such responses may not come naturally. Consequently, it is a good practice to provide training and assistance to all district administrators and to staff whose responsibility it is to work with the media. In fact, Houston (1993) suggests that administrators ought to take an example from those whom we call "spinmeisters" in current political parlance. In layman's terms, Houston suggests that it is important not to leave the "spin" to others but rather to simply present facts and information in an understandable manner and in a manner that disseminates the school district's story.

According to Houston, the message district administrators wish to convey must be repeated in order to be absorbed and remembered by the general public. Schools and districts should respond to questions the public is asking and address concerns identified by their constituents, both in the school and at the district level, and should do that in a truthful manner, one which facilitates trust building. Sally Zakariya (1987) suggested in an article that a reporter's trust is violated when the whole truth is not told (p. 19). Once that trust is gone, it is almost impossible to regain.

Other suggestions that assist in building a strong, positive relationship with the media, and through the media with patrons and other constituents, include:

- Be available.
- Return reporter's calls.
- Don't say "no comment" (Knight in Zakariya, 1987, p. 20).

Larry Zenke (1987), who has had significant experience as a superintendent, noted in his writing that admitting mistakes, researching answers to questions for which you initially have no answers, and treating members of the press as professionals are important aspects of good media relations as well (p. 21). Like it or not, education relies on the media to convey its story much the same way the media relies on educators and educational systems for much of the news. The relationship may be symbiotic or synergistic. The determination of what the relationship will be is largely up to the superintendent, board, and district administrators.

IMPACT OF CENTRAL OFFICE MEDIA SKILLS

Behavior of top administrators and the expectations they convey relative to the entire question of public relations and media relations in particular will be emulated throughout the district. It is not only interviews and responses to phone calls that convey the message of the district, however. A simple act of communication such as answering the phone can tell much about the public relations and attitudes of district leadership as reflected in employee attitudes. Tone of voice conveys attitude as much as body language and facial expression do. The impact on a caller of a negative tone of voice or surly response cannot be overestimated. The caller may be a member of the press or a patron. In either case, there is no way to recapture lost good feelings brought about by a fractious tone, a moment of anger, or contentiousness in answering a phone call or responding to a query.

The role of central administration in relation to such negative possibilities is to ensure that adequate training is provided to all staff who will deal with the public or respond to public concerns. Additionally, all administrators should monitor staff behaviors relative to public relations and correct inappropriate behaviors as necessary.

Every staff member should have access to a procedures handbook that clearly delineates the roles each individual should play relative to public relations and in all other aspects of school operations as they relate to the particular job responsibilities the person has. In fact, it is an excellent idea to engage staff in the development of a procedures manual that reflects and flows from the policy book of the district as well as appropriate state law and district regulations. The procedures manual can be updated on a regular basis as policies are changed and relevant law or legal decisions are affected. Sections contained in the procedures manual should be job-related, should clearly show lines of authority, and should reflect the district vision and mission. Among the sections that should be included are procedures concerning

- communications during regular school activities and during emergency situations
- procedures for notification from school sites to the central office during emergencies
- procedures for involving the police in response to school events
- procedures for responses to the media and designations of key communicators that designate proper authority for providing responses

Although the procedures manual should be all-encompassing and the topics listed are generally limited to issues that may involve contact with the media and the public, there are other concerns that arise in which the public has interest and which demand good public relations skills. Among these are student attendance policy and procedures, student discipline policy and procedures, policy and procedures related to student participation in extracurricular activities, and staff employment, promotion, and termination policy and procedures.

Of course, the superintendent would wish to involve staff at all levels in the development of the procedures materials and to keep the board updated and knowledgeable about the process. As the policy makers, board members have a vested interest in all aspects of school functioning. As stakeholders, all staff can provide perspectives and information that may not be accessible to the central office staff or to principals but should certainly be factored into a valid development and presentation of procedures.

PASSING A MILLAGE: THE ULTIMATE PR TEST

When a new millage is necessary for construction of facilities or for the general operations of a school district, it is not possible to build much public support. The campaign to pass a millage will succeed or fail based on the existence or lack of existence of support gain prior to the decision to raise millages. Millage increases are tantamount to raising taxes. Few people, if any, actually desire a tax increase. Consequently, the decision to seek a millage increase and the resultant campaign will focus not on garnering goodwill but on encouraging those who already have a positive image of the district to vote for the proposal.

The millage campaign is geared primarily to a three-pronged process of notification of needs, justification for the requested mills, and voter encouragement. In some states and districts, millage elections are held concurrently with the general election. In such cases, the district and its campaign committee need only to explain the request for additional taxes and tell the voters to look for the issue on the ballot. In states and districts where school elections are held at a different time from the normal general elections, a more intensive effort to provide public notice is necessary to ensure even a modest voter turnout. Naturally, a good relationship with the press is helpful with notification, for it enhances the probability that coverage will be adequate and well-placed within the print media and news-broadcast formats. Superintendent appearances on radio and television talk shows can also assist with the justification efforts.

JUSTIFICATION

Part of the public relations work associated with a millage effort must be focused on justification. As noted, few persons actually want to pay more taxes. Accordingly, a need must be justified, which will cause patrons of the district to vote positively for the proposed issue. Teachers and other school and district staff must also believe that there is a need to support the millage.

In fact teachers, staff and students are crucial to the passage of a millage. They are important because they influence other voters and in most cases can vote themselves. (At least, this is true of staff and teachers who live within the district and are registered voters.) Their influence extends beyond the period immediately around election time, however. The demeanor and comments of teachers and students as well as other district staff carry much weight within the community and therefore may be determining factors in the election results.

The created need or justification for a new or increased millage will come about by means of communications from the district and its personnel. If buildings are to be constructed or remodeled, it is helpful to have a model of the new or renovated facility available for public viewing. If the millage is for repairs, a list of schools and specific projects should be made available to the public and to district employees alike. If the millage is to enhance the general fund, maintenance, and operations budget, an explanation should be provided for the use of the dollars to be raised. Pie charts and other visual devices published in the newspaper can be helpful for conveying this information. The board, the superintendent, and other district employees should be knowledgeable and available to respond to questions and public concerns with regard to the millage requests and the prospective use of dollars generated.

VOTER ENCOURAGEMENT

Planning is important in the daily public relations activities of a district and a school. It is even more important in the attempt to pass a millage. Care should be taken to understand and address the concerns of those who oppose the bond issue. It is a good practice to include individuals from all major interest groups in the community as participants in the planning process and in the millage effort. The timing of release of information for publication should be planned, and every effort must be made to get ahead of the rumor mill in relation to daily events in the district.

CAVEATS

There are a few warnings which must be issued in relation to public relations and particularly in regard to millage campaigns. It is possible in the intensive quest for positive patron support to momentarily forget the responsibility the district has for the education of students and the good stewardship of public dollars.

When planning and conducting a campaign, ensure that no public money is used and that employee time is after work hours and is voluntary. District stationery must not be used; in fact, a wise superintendent and board organizes a campaign committee that includes no district personnel and that generates its own funding from money raised by members of that committee.

Teachers must be educated with regard to possible issues that might arise within the campaign as well. On more than one occasion, a committed teacher has used the millage effort as an opportunity to encourage parents to vote and as an English lesson as well. The use of class time for political purposes has been roundly criticized. The assignment that required students to write letters to parents and grandparents urging support of a millage with which some parents disagreed received even more criticism. Unfortunately, such ill-conceived but well-intentioned activities may negatively impact election outcomes while simultaneously making the teachers a target of public derision.

District and school administrators would be well advised to warn teachers of such potentialities and to suggest that if they want to show support for a millage effort, their vote and voluntary assistance are important.

ADDITIONAL SUGGESTIONS FOR DAILY
PUBLIC RELATIONS ACTIVITIES

Public relations, like other district functions, must receive daily attention. Newsletters, staff appreciation days, student appreciation activities, public opportunities for use of school facilities, and public invitations to student concerts and plays are all good devices for the building of positive perceptions with regard to schools.

However, the best assurance of public support continues to be predicated on student achievement, appropriate use of public money, and positive school climates where students and teachers can work in safety. There is no substitute for a quality education in the eye of the public. That is what most school patrons remember from their own experience, and it is what most school patrons expect for their children. Schools and districts that provide that quality education will experience support, and positive public relations will be a concomitant of that support.

REFERENCES

Derrington, M. L. (February 1993). "Calming controversy." *The Executive Educator.* 15: 32–34.

Elam, S. M. & Rose, L. C. (October 1995). "The 27th annual Phi Delta Kappa/Gallup Poll." *Kappan.* 77: 41–56.

Houston, P. (June 1993). "Be your own spin doctor." *The Executive Educator.* 15: 15.

Roles and relationships: School boards and superintendents. (1994). Arlington, VA: The American Association of School Administrators.

Yukl, G. A. & Tracey, J. B. (1992). Consequences of influence tactics used with subordinates, peers, and the boss. *Journal of Applied Psychology.* 77(44): 525–535.

Zakariya, S. B. (August, 1987). "Extra: Three news pros tell how to score with the press." *The Executive Educator.* 9: 19–20.

Zenke, L. L. (August, 1987). "Creamed by the press? Try this media relations recipe." *The Executive Educator.* 9: 21,30.

CHAPTER 12

Legal Aspects of Central Administration

Legal issues arise on a daily basis within the context of school administration. There are few activities that can divert the attention of teachers and administrators from their educational responsibilities to a greater degree. However, with appropriate training in place, there are few aspects of administration and teaching which can be so easily resolved.

AMONG the most challenging aspects of school administration and board service is address to legal issues. Although most superintendents and board members are not attorneys, a thorough knowledge of the law, as it relates to education, is essential for successful day-to-day district operations. Principals, too, must have a thorough grounding in legal precedent and processes. Perhaps in the past general knowledge of constitutional law may have been sufficient for effective administration, but those days are gone. In an increasingly litigious society, it is not only the general public but also professionals, including educators, who seek redress of actual or perceived wrongs through the courts.

CONSTITUTIONAL ISSUES

There continues to be legal precedent for the protection of student rights in public education and for the property and liberty interests parents have in the acquisition of a quality education for their children. Public schools and, consequently, public school administrators and teachers must operate within these parameters even though courts have tended to support the reasoned and reasonable decisions of school authorities in litigation during the past decade.

Private schools operate generally on a contractual basis although those private institutions that accept federal assistance do have some specific requirements they must meet by virtue of that aid. This means that students attending private schools and the parents of such students have a contract with the private school. Violation of the contract, including disciplinary expectations, will result normally in expulsion of the student based on contractual breach. Generally, private schools are not impacted by all federal law unless they receive federal aid through Chapter/Title I or other federal programs.

Legal precedent addresses discipline, student expression, academic freedom, religion in the schools, school-associated activities, and due process. As the law develops through court decisions within the state, within the region (circuit), and in the Supreme Court, it behooves the superintendent and board not only to keep abreast of new judicial opinions but also to advise and to educate teachers and other administrators as well.

Although most administrators have taken course work in school law, some may not have completed courses or updated their knowledge bases in several years. It is important to know the content of several precedent-setting decisions. They are listed here and discussed in this brief in this chapter.

Ingraham v. Wright, Goss v. Lopez, and the T. L. O. case (*New Jersey v. T.L.O.*) are but a few of the cases with which all administrators and school boards should be familiar. Whether or not the board and district retain an attorney, it is advisable for some legal knowledge to be available in the repertoire of the board and the administrators it employs. This is true not only because there are so many situations in which such knowledge is crucial but also, more important, because the attorney, whether on a retainer or operating on a fee basis, will not always be available to the particular board member or administrator when questions of due process or legal precedent arise. Additionally, as a school district moves closer to site-based management, the school administrators will be expected to be able to address difficult situations faced by staff and students as well as patrons with less and less dependence on central administrators.

While such independence does not preclude seeking advice or asking for clarification, it is generally expected that the school administrator possesses the skills and expertise to do the job which has been given to him or her. Of course, this is precisely why some school administrators have been reluctant to accept school-based management as an appropriate district practice. School-based management, as noted earlier in the text, requires that the school administrator be accountable, even when some accountability lies with central administration. The other side of the coin is that school-based management places authority in the hands of school site administrators and ostensibly lessens the control that the superintendent and/or central administration has over daily decisions. This includes decisions that have legal ramifications not only for the principal or assistant principal but also for the district administration and school board.

ADMINISTRATION OF PUNISHMENT

Ingraham v. Wright is a 1977 case in which the courts spoke to the issue of corporal punishment. The question of law in this case was whether or not corporal punishment violates the Eighth Amendment, which addresses "cruel or unusual punishment," or Fourteenth Amendment due process. While the Supreme Court found that corporal punishment does not violate in and of itself, this 1977 case and other cases have clearly delineated the fact that harsh or severe corporal punishment may violate the Eighth and/or Fourteenth Amendments.

Decisions in circuit cases have suggested some basic parameters relative to corporal punishment that are applicable in circuits, states, and school districts where corporal punishment is allowed. Among the conditions addressed are the relative sizes of the punished and punisher, the emotional state of the individual administering the punishment, gender issues, the number of strokes appropriately given, the age of the child or student, and the instrument used for administration of the punishment.

It is not sufficient to know that corporal punishment is permissible in some circumstances. It is also important for the administrator to be aware of the case law that applies within his or her circuit and federal judicial district. It is likewise crucial that the school district and school comply with the state regulations in regard to administration of such punishment and with reference to due process for the student being punished.

In the situation of a student who is placed in isolation until his or her unacceptable behavior changes, the courts have not had a problem with removal of the child from the classroom or with the concept of detention, but most jurists would find that placement of a child in a "time out" box or in a closet may represent the tort of false imprisonment. Teachers and administrators must be aware of such likelihood in the administration of discipline. They should also be aware of the personal and civil consequences of such behavior as it may result in a monetary judgment against the individual who perpetrated the isolation or "false imprisonment tort" as well as the administrator who condoned it.

For both teachers and students due process is a major issue in and of itself in the administration of discipline. The Fourteenth Amendment to the United States Constitution guarantees due process, that is, the protection of life, liberty, and property under the law in actions taken by the state. The school district is a creature of the state, and school district officials are agents of the state. Due process is both procedural and substantive.

Procedural due process refers to the processes followed, for example: Was the student/teacher notified of his or her rights in a timely manner and of the charges against him or her? Was there a chance to confront witnesses? Was the teacher/student advised of appeal rights? Was the hearing conducted by an impartial person?

Substantive due process rights relate to the interest the individual student or teacher has in an education or employment situation, respectively, and whether or not that interest is violated by the action of the administrator. When punishment is administered, due process rights must be respected and accorded the teacher or students. It is imperative that teachers, administrators, school board members, and patrons be aware of and knowledgeable about these rights and that due process is followed.

Of course, due process is constitutionally protected. In a school district, however, time is money, and money is in short supply. The failure of teachers and/or administrators to afford due process rights may result in the loss of both, as the district attempts to defend its actions in hearings and in court. In restructuring districts, as more authority is given to the school site and its personnel, an education in the law is crucial to ensure defensible decisions and appropriate compliance with legal precedent and requirements. Not only is awareness of due process important but also the choice of penalty and manner of administration of that penalty, which may play a significant role in whether or not a student's rights have been violated and whether or not the penalty and the process used in applying the penalty will be upheld on appeal.

SEARCH AND SEIZURE

The major school-related cases in the area of search and seizure are *New Jersey v. T.L.O.* and *O'Connor v. Ortega.* The former deals with student search and the latter with privacy rights and search issues relative to employees. The standard of "reasonable suspicion," which applies in schools, is delineated in the T.L.O. case. As most administrators are aware, the standard for police is "probable cause," a stricter standard.

In cases involving students or those involving teachers, the expectation of privacy is an issue to be considered. An item left in plain view is not considered to have any privacy expectation associated with it. The same is true of a lost purse, briefcase, or backpack. It is reasonable to expect the opening of a lost container in order to ascertain ownership and to ensure return to the item's owner. Consequently, any contraband items found therein are not subject to Fourth Amendment protections against unlawful search and seizure. Other items may not be "legally searchable" without reasonable suspicion.

It is important that teachers and administrators be familiar with the court's standards in these two cases as they work with each other and with students.

> The doctrine formulated in T.L.O. limits searches to situations that meet the following conditions: (1.) A *school official* must have (2.) *reasonable grounds* to believe that (3.) a search of a specific individual will produce (4.) *relevant evidence* that the individual has violated a (5.) *specific school rule or law.* (Imber & Van Geel, 1995, p. 68).

In the case of teachers, although there is protection under the Fourth Amendment in regard to searches and seizures and although the rule with regard to plain view and lost purses, briefcases, and so on applies, the issue of privacy is somewhat unclear. It is generally held that a supervisor may look in a teacher's desk or file cabinet for materials—for example, gradebooks—that are necessary to conduct daily business. (Certainly, if a substitute is in the class, that substitute must have a copy of the gradebook and pertinent lesson plans in order to teach effectively.)

If in the context of the search something indicative of a violation of a work-related rule or a law is found—for example a packet of drugs—the search may still be deemed to be reasonable. There are limitations on such searches; for example, an expectation of privacy normally exists in a school with reference to areas that are locked and to which *only* the individual employee or teacher, by practice and expectation, has access absent permission from the teacher or employee.

It is important that teachers and administrators be aware of these issues not only for their own protection but also so that as they interact with each other and with students, appropriate procedures are followed. With an increasing move toward site-based management, school site personnel will be more and more accountable in these matters. In order to avoid mistakes and liability and to protect rights, the knowledge of appropriate actions and decisions must be available to all of these employees. There must be an overriding educational justification for school officials to violate the reasonable expectation of privacy that teachers do have (McCarthy & Cambron-McCabe, 1995).

Other circumstances in which the courts have held that searches are not intrusive are in situations in which student safety may be at stake. For example, bus drivers may be tested for drugs predicated on the fact that they operate equipment that is dangerous and that they are responsible for the safety of students whom they drive to and from school and other activities.

RIGHTS OF SPEECH, EXPRESSION, PRESS, AND RELIGION

During the decade of the 1970s, issues of expression were the focus of much attention in the courts and in the press. Cases such as *Hazelwood v. Kuhlmeier* and the key student expression case, *Tinker v. Des Moines,* caught national attention. The decisions in these cases and others have applicability to educational practice today. Issues of student expression continue to arise as school boards and school employees attempt to address student dress, language, and the advent of gang behaviors in schools.

In these cases, as in those mentioned relative to search and seizure as well as cases that will be referenced in following sections, the courts have established "tests" that may be applied in order to determine the appropriateness and legality of specific administrative actions. The questions an administrator must ask prior to censoring student publications and/or prior to imposing dress or grooming regulations are:

(1) Does the behavior (dress, writing, etc.) represent a material interference or a substantial disruption of the educational process, the school's routine?

(2) Does the behavior or writing substantially interfere with the rights of other students?

There is case law that addresses the behavior and dress of teachers and other employees as well. In *East Hartford Education Association v. Board of Education of Town of East Hartford,* which was decided in the Second Circuit but which may be considered persuasive in other circuits, the school board was able to regulate teacher dress. In this particular case, a teacher refused to comply with a dress regulation requiring the wearing of a necktie by male teachers instructing students in core academic subjects. The teacher alleged a violation of his right of free expression. The court held that a school board may impose *reasonable* regulations on the appearance of the teachers whom it employs in order to meet the educational goals within the district.

Other areas of teacher rights that courts have addressed and of which teachers and administrators must be apprised include but are not limited to:

- speech rights: When can a teacher speak out against the district or personnel within the district? The answer relates to public versus private criticism and the public's need to know.
- teacher property interest in the job: What are the rights and due process necessary for discipline, termination, or nonrenewal of probationary and nonprobationary teachers?
- teacher behavior within the community: In some instances teacher behavior deemed inappropriate within the context of community mores has been held to be grounds for termination. In other circumstances and communities, this has not been the case.
- academic freedom: This legal concept may or may not extend to religious expression by the teacher, but it does include attention to the expertise of the teacher, the age of the student, the inappropriateness of obscene or pornographic materials, the use of curse words in class, and instruction outside of the recognized field of teacher expertise.
- teacher religious expression: This includes dress, the wearing of religious ornaments or symbols, the presence of religious materials in the classroom, and an examination of the conditions under which religious concepts and history may and may not be taught in the classroom or school. This area of litigation also extends to teacher behavior with students, for example prayer at extracurricular activities, in assemblies, or "around the flagpole."

It would be wise for every administrator to attend periodic "refresher" staff development in regard to each of these issues and to provide such training for teachers as well.

FINANCE AND DESEGREGATION

Although ostensibly the issues surrounding school finance and desegregation, generally supposed to be equity, equality, adequacy, and quality, are concerns that should be uppermost in the minds of all educators, this is not always the case. However, teachers and administrators should be informed about this area of the law.

For example, the concept of special education, which was discussed in Chapter 8 of this text, requires that special effort be made to assist those students who are at a disadvantage in the learning process due to mental and/or physical disabilities. That assistance is largely an equity issue. Students who are disadvantaged by socioeconomic status and achievement level may receive the benefit of special effort through the Chapter/Title 1 programs in school districts. That too is an equity issue. Students whose socioeconomic disadvantage is such that they do not have adequate family income to support them in terms of health and nutrition benefit from the school lunch programs. This support has been in place nationally since 1946.

In school districts that operate under the aegis of either the federal courts or a desegregation plan or both, administrators and teachers must be similarly concerned with providing a quality adequate education for all students. Efforts should be made to ensure that the equity needs of students are met and that the parameters established in the desegregation plan or court order are factored in to the planning, support, and educational processes of the district.

It is the responsibility of the school board and the superintendent and his staff to assure equity in distribution of funds and other resources to schools within the district. It is the responsibility of the principal to ensure equitable allocations of funds at the school level. Finance issues generally focus on state funding formulae and their impact on districts rather than on the distribution of dollars within districts among schools. Teachers and administrators should be cognizant of their responsibilities in the realm of equity, however. It is natural and expected that each teacher and administrator seeks to maximize funding within the district and in terms of personal income. However, an understanding of the exigencies within which state school officers and central office administrators must operate will help all within a district focus their attention on maximizing the education of all students with appropriate and effective use of the resources available rather than wasting energy on complaints or discontent relative to resources that are not available to the district or the school. Communication within the district is crucial in attaining this end.

The role of superintendent and indeed of all educators is to provide such understandings to patrons, board members, other administrators, and teachers.

DAILY OPERATIONS AND LEGAL QUESTIONS

It is important to remember that teachers typically have little or no training in educational law or in law in general. Consequently, concerns arise on a regular basis relative to employment conditions, contracts, agency, and individual liability. The school administration as well as district administrators should be able to respond to such questions, if not with definitive legal information then at least with knowledge as to where the answers to legal queries might be obtained.

The purview of the law extends to all areas of educational practice. Legal precedent (court cases), laws (legislative codes), and regulations cover virtually every activity within the schools. Extracurricular activities, teacher duties in instruction and supervision, opportunities for male and female students, curriculum standards, child abuse and the reporting responsibilities of educators relative to it, and the construction and use of school district buildings or property are among the legal concerns that have been affected by case law.

School administrators must have some legal knowledge in each of these areas. If adminstrators and teachers are not familiar with the specifics of each pertinent legal decision, there should at least be familiarity with methods to access such legal requirements and case law in order to appropriately inform decisions.

It is strongly suggested that the school district maintain a teachers/administrators legal materials center to help administrators and teachers locate up-to-date information on legal issues. This should be in addition to the previously suggested staff development in school law and the availability of legal advice from a practicing attorney who specializes in school law.

REFERENCES

Camp, W. E., Underwood, J. K., Connelly, M. J. & Lane, K. E. (eds.) (1993). *The principal's legal handbook.* Topeka, KS: NOLPE.

Champion, W. T. (1993). *Sports law.* St. Paul, MN: West Publishing Co.

East Hartford Education Association v. Board of Education of Town of East Hartford, 562 F.2d. 838 (1977).

Hazelwood v. Kuhlmeier, 484 U.S. 260 (1988).

Imber, M. & van Geel, T. (1995). *A teacher's guide to education law.* NY: McGraw-Hill.

Ingraham v. Wright, 430 U.S. 651 (1977).

LaMorte, M.W. (1996). *School law: Cases and concepts.* (5th ed.) Boston: Allyn & Bacon.

McCarthy, M. M. & Cambron-McCabe, N. H. (1995) *Public school law: Teachers' and students' rights.* (3rd Ed.) Boston: Allyn & Bacon.

New Jersey v. T.L.O., 469 U.S. 325 (1985).

O'Connor v. Ortega, 480 U.S.209 (1987).

Rossow, L. F. & Stefkovich, J. A. (1995). *Search and seizure in the public schools.* Topeka, KS: NOLPE.

Tinker v. Des Moines, 393 U.S. 503 (1969).

Zirkel, P. A., Richardson, S. N. & Goldberg, S. S. (1995). *A digest of Supreme Court decisions affecting education.* (3rd ed.) Bloomington, IN: Phi Delta Kappa.

CHAPTER 13

The New Roles: Central Administration Redefined by Law and Practice

Philosophical, social, and cultural changes within society in general and schools in particular demand changes in the structure of schools and school districts and their address to the needs of children.

RESTRUCTURING THE DISTRICT

ONE of the most difficult tasks any central office administrator will undertake is the seemingly simple act of proposing a restructuring of a district or of a program. The thought of restructuring the entire district will send thrills of joy through some people and cause others to experience great consternation.

The reasons for such diverse responses are really quite simple. For some individuals, the idea of change is abhorrent, as change in organizational structure requires them to change behaviors and habits. For others, change can carry heavy costs. It may cost them the positions they have held and in which they have achieved a certain level of comfort, that is, mastery of the tasks to be performed, without significant effort. For still others, the thought and challenge of change gives pause as change represents a movement into unknown responsibilities and the acceptance of new ideas. Yet that is what makes the possibility of change intriguing.

Restructuring is far more than adding or deleting certain positions, however. Restructuring cannot be cosmetic. It implies planning, building bases for agreement and decision making predicated not only on the district mission but also on a vision of what the district and the schools therein should be. Restructuring must be a *process*. It is surely not a product as it must be ongoing. The implication is that the organization is

127

a living entity and as such it must respond to the needs of the changing society in which it exists while simultaneously guarding and maintaining values, curricula, and practices that are foundational and essential for the appropriate education of students.

So defined, restructuring is rather like reengineering in business management terms, that is, "redesigning the organization's core processes by essentially starting with a blank sheet of paper . . . ignoring the way things have historically been done and completely redesigning everything the organization does" (Robbins, 1997, p. 529). Such reengineering is time-consuming and nerveracking. It demands consensus building and team building. Ownership by all constituents is key if changes are to be internalized and eventually institutionalized.

Resistance to change often arises not only from individuals but also from interest groups within the community. The more diverse the community, the higher the likelihood that change proposals will meet resistance. Consequently, prior to any change, but particularly in situations in which restructuring is taking place, various individuals and their constituencies must be ready for the reengineering or change being contemplated. Readiness is predicated on laying a groundwork within each constituency by means of planning, involvement, and effective communication.

The social, political, and economic effects of change do indeed impact the priorities of each community group within a school district (Kahne, 1996). In order to work effectively with each constituency, the leadership team must be able to diagnose the readiness stage at which each stakeholder group may be, ascertaining whether each group is willing and able (Hersey, Blanchard & Johnson, 1996) to engage in the change process. To assess this readiness level, the following questions may be asked:

- Is each constituency or key player able to understand what is actually happening in the district and the effectiveness of the extant district structure?
- Is each constituency or key player able to visualize that which must happen to facilitate reaching the new vision?
- Does each individual have the information necessary to weigh the pros and cons of the change?
- Are adequate time and resources available to facilitate a planning process that can lead to change predicated not on compromise but rather on consensus?
- Has the discussion, debate, or exchange of information and

concerns been rational? If so, there doubtless is some understanding of the need for restructuring and some commitment to it. If not, more time and discussion are necessary using language and experiences that are understood by the particular constituency and reflective of its concerns.

- Have adequate training and planning time been given to those who will be asked to change and to those whose responsibility it is to initiate changes?

REALIGNING RESPONSIBILITIES

For district personnel, the realignment of responsibilities that generally accompanies any change process is particularly threatening. One of the first heard and most consistent objections to change is to be found in the phrase "but we've always done it this way." Realignment of responsibilities means the loss of some responsibilities and the acquisition of others. Personal preference is rarely the basis on which such shifts are made. Rather, the process of reengineering for site-based management may mean the reconfiguration of reporting relationships, a change in line and staff authority, and learning or reinforcing management and leadership skills.

For example, in school districts that have organizational structures featuring a separation of curriculum and instruction, that is, an associate or assistant superintendent for each, the two educational functions may be combined. In school districts, regardless of size, where the central administration has traditionally been housed at one site, the relocation of personnel into the schools may improve both communication and collegiality. It will also cause initial discomfort both to the principal and teachers at the school site and to the central administrator who is relocated, particularly if he or she has not been in direct contact with students for some time. The focus of the school district must be on the student and student achievement, however. What better way to focus on students than to move services closer to them?

The presence of students in the daily interactive life of the central office administrator, coupled with constant contact with teachers and principals, can and should help focus central office personnel on the reason they are in the school business. It will also test and put to rest time-honored but archaic theories and responses that have evolved over the years but which are not relevant to the community and students the school district is attempting to serve today. Finally, the experience of working hand in glove with school site personnel will revalidate theories and experience that are pertinent to the clientele being served and to the true community needs and issues, be they fiscal, disciplinary, curricular, instructional, or some combination of these.

If neither realignment nor redefinition of responsibilities can be taken lightly, then restructuring must be understood by all and implemented with maximal involvement from all constituencies. The vision of the superintendent and school board should be understood by all. Each constituency and each individual within the district must either commit to make the changes successful or at least agree not to stand in the way of change.

Restructuring involves an alteration in attitude that recognizes that education, as currently provided to students, does not work for many and that therefore a different experience must be given them (Lewis, 1989). Restructuring must be accomplished with a focus on the students served not only by the district but also by each school within the district. For example, a school that serves a preponderance of lower socioeconomic students can and should develop a different culture and goal focus from that developed for schools whose clients are primarily middle-class or upper-class socioeconomically. The needs of each group of students may be similar in terms of curriculum, but they definitely vary in terms of instructional approaches and the form in which the curriculum is delivered.

NEW POSITIONS/NEW CONCERNS

To address the clientele served by means of site-based management within each school and district, the organizational chart must change significantly. Reporting relationships and responsibilities must reflect the priorities within the schools and communities served. The organizational chart should be flattened, thereby removing unnecessary bureaucratic layers between the school principal and the superintendent. Consequently, management areas that may have been configured as units—for example, a division of curriculum and instruction—may be subdivided, thereby allowing curriculum specialists to be assigned to particular schools to which they provide exclusive service.

In large districts, assistant superintendents may be moved into schools and given support by an assigned cadre of curriculum supervisors in mathematics, language arts/English, social studies, and science. Additional assistance may be provided by staff assigned from a division of research and monitoring. These individuals would be advisors to principals in a subdistrict and would work with the assistant superintendent to provide support to the schools in that subdistrict. This arrangement would create a manageable span of control for central office administrators, provide more immediate and direct assistance to principals and teachers at the school sites, and ensure that some central office staff are very familiar with the needs, strengths, and culture of every school.

Moderate-sized districts may opt for a similar structure that encourages central office and school site teaming. In a sense, the assignment of a core group of individuals to work directly within a geographical area of the school district and with a particular set of schools will have the impact of rejoining curricular and instructional personnel with those who are responsible for the day-to-day teaching and administrative operations of the district. Additionally, if geographic zones are created and schools are grouped, it is suggested that the grouping reflect student movement from elementary to middle level (or junior high) and then to high school. There is much power in facilitating the opportunity for principals and teachers from the various levels to plan together and to share the vision and nuances of the educational process for a cohort of students who generally move together from level to level. Additionally, discipline and student self-concepts are positively impacted when these students have the opportunity to progress with a cadre of friends as they move to the next educational level.

Small school districts have no need to reconfigure geographically in such a manner. Neither will they find it necessary to redivide responsibilities, since generally there is not an assistant superintendent or, if there is, that individual tends to deal with the exigencies of both administration (day-to-day operations) *and* curriculum. There is, however, a need to refocus efforts in many small districts and to redefine the sharing of responsibilities among superintendent, assistant superintendent, and principals. Oddly, even in some districts that have as few as two or three schools, the central administration is housed in separate buildings and functions as a "headquarters," giving directives and direction with little school site collaboration.

In medicine, it is generally the primary care physician who conducts a preliminary diagnosis and determines whether or not the client needs further intervention. In schools, too, those closest to the clients (students) must be the primary diagnosticians and must have the latitude, based on expertise, to prescribe programs and methods to address problems. This is the value of and basis for site-based management. As the specialist collaborates with the primary care physician and communicates with him or her, so too the central office administrator and curriculum specialists or fiscal officers should work collaboratively with principals and teachers at the school sites. Such synergistic associations can maximize both personnel and resources and their impact on the education of students.

UNRESOLVED ISSUES

Middle level education, student discipline and safety, student achievement, fiscal responsibility, and equity are issues faced in common by educators today. Although these are not the only issues of concern, they are sufficiently important to have captured national attention. In each case, policy may be effected at the district (superintendent and board) level, but the actual implementation of strategic planning to address each issue must take place at the school site. If it is true that people tend to support that which they create, then planning and change in relation to all concerns must take place at the school site. The new role for central administration in light of this is to provide support, guidance, and assistance *as needed.*

A fundamental stumbling block for many central office administrators will be loss of power or authority. An understanding of the theory base with regard to both power and authority can help allay those fears. Although school and district administrators may not be consciously aware of it, power and authority issues permeate most aspects of school activity. The title an administrator is given affects relationships even if the person holding the position has only held the particular job for a matter of hours. The perceptions of former colleagues tend to change based on their understanding of the new power or authority that the manager or administrator has acquired.

Authority is not only legal, informal, and formal but may also be functional, that is, based on the competence of the individual. Informal authority stems from the behavior and attributes of an individual. Formal authority stems from the position held.

Power, on the other hand, may be legitimate, that is, based on a formal position held. It may also be referent. Referent power is predicated on the administrator's ability and the subordinate's identification with the administrator. Coercive power is power based on the fear or apprehension of punishment of the subordinate. Expert power relates to the knowledge that the leader is perceived to possess (Hoy & Miskel, 1991).

Generally, administrative knowledge and behavior patterns speak for themselves. It is not necessary to exert authority or to remind others of individual power. Those with whom the central office administrators work will recognize that both power and authority bases exist and will decide whether to be respectful of them based on the value of assistance provided and/or the interpersonal relation skills possessed by that administrator. The community will tend to respond from a similar perspective and in a similar fashion.

AFFIRMATIVE ACTION AND LABOR RELATIONS

As recently as ten years ago, it was not necessary to focus on a regular basis on issues such as teacher strikes, employee-to-employee harassment, and Title IX and Title VI disputes in school districts. At the present time, however, such issues arise in districts of all sizes fairly consistently. Consequently, it is important that restructuring districts ensure that there is an individual on staff who can assist in addressing such issues. Affirmative action in practice must be monitored within the district. A central office administrator whose responsibility it is to work with human resources (personnel) must be knowledgeable in this area.

In an increasing number of districts, teachers and other staff are seeking to unionize or form associations that are tantamount to unions. Labor relations skills are important not only in the process of contract negotiations but also in conducting grievance hearings, fact finding, mediation, and working with the National Labor Relations Board and its corps of possible arbitrators and mediators.

As noted by Geisert and Lieberman (1994), "the consequences of not being prepared [for negotiations and dealing with employee bargaining units] are loss of management prerogatives, loss of flexibility, increased public dissatisfaction, greater uniformity, and excessive operating costs" (p. xi). Not only is it important to identify and train an individual to address labor issues but it is also crucial to structure a central office team of people with shared understandings who are effective and knowledgeable in responding to these issues.

DESEGREGATION OFFICERS, MONITORS, AND EQUITY

School districts in several states are engaged in the process of desegregating their schools. Some districts have obtained unitary status but must operate within guidelines set through litigation. Still other districts have experienced changes in school funding at the state, local, and federal levels that have affected their ability to fund instruction and special programs for students in need of specific assistance or remediation. No matter which scenario has impacted or is affecting a district and its administrators, focus on the key issue, the education of children, must not be lost in the restructuring process or in the press to desegregate or to provide educational equity.

As in the case of affirmative action, the district must have an individual who provides leadership and fulfills a monitoring and assistance function relative to equity and desegregation. This person should be available to provide training and focus to school administrators and staffs as well. There is no requirement that the school equity officer be located at the central office or that he or she be a central office administrator, although it may be easier for the equity officer to maintain an objective view if he or she is not on the staff at a particular school.

Nonetheless, the role and responsibilities of this individual must center around linking daily activities and the district/school vision to the goal of providing equity and excellence in the educational process for every child. It is so easy in the press of daily activity to lose sight of the need to teach *each child* and to provide the supports necessary to ensure that *each child* does learn. This staff member functioning as the equity officer may assist the teams that work with schools in the monitoring of student achievement and disaggregation of data in order to assess whether or not the educational needs of all students, regardless of race and gender, are being met.

THE DECISION TO RESTRUCTURE

Restructuring does not occur simply because one individual or a board envisions such change. Reengineering is a long-term, ongoing process that must engage all constituents and every employee of the district. It must be predicated on a vision of what can be and must be grounded in a realistic assessment of where the district and its schools are, where they need to be, and how they can reach that goal.

Organizational health must be factored into the process. In fact, there are several Organizational Health Inventories available to help assess morale, resource utilization, communication adequacy, institutional integrity in the face of community interests, and the other components of a healthy organization. (These terms vary from instrument to instrument but the concepts undergirding them are consistent.) Such a survey can provide the district with a realistic view of where it is in terms of many important issues and parameters. If that view is compared to where the district must be in order to provide an adequate, efficient education for all students, the process steps for reaching the vision will emerge and can be linked to a timeline for accomplishment of the steps. Additionally, responsibilities may be identified and collaboration toward change can begin.

Restructuring cannot be a nebulous process. Certainly, change is difficult, as previously noted. However, often it is the lack of planning and direction that is most unsettling. With a road map and adequate resources, most people are willing to embark on a journey, even if it involves significant transformations.

ASKING REASONABLE QUESTIONS

There is a series of questions that each constituency, including school staffs, central administration, and the school board, must ask in order to determine whether or not change is needed and how to make appropriate changes in order to restructure for equity and excellence.

Data Gathering: Data must be gathered in order to ascertain what the district is accomplishing vis à vis its students.

(1) What is the achievement level of students in the district by race and gender as measured by standardized tests?

(2) What is the comparative position of the district in relation to other districts within the state and the national average as measured by standardized tests?

(3) What is the district dropout rate?

(4) What percentage of students obtain employment upon graduation?

(5) What percentage of students attend a two-year, four-year, or vocational institution upon graduation?

(6) What rating do employers give the education received by the students who have graduated from the district? (poor, average, above average, excellent)

(7) What rating do graduates from the district give the education they received after they have been away from the district for five years?

(8) What percentage of district graduates require remediation upon completion of school in order to be successful in college or technical school?

Internal and External Data-Based Goal Setting:

(1) What is the district goal in terms of each of these areas:
student achievement
student retention
student employability
student ability to succeed in higher education

(2) What is the community goal in terms of these areas?

From the answers to these and other questions that may be unique to a district or community, a vision and a plan can emerge that will become the basis for effective and ongoing restructuring. The caveat is that a commitment must be made and effected to change the process for delivery of services to students, moving that process closer to the school and the student and empowering those who work directly with students. Only in this way can successful systemic educational change occur.

REFERENCES

Geisert, G. & Lieberman, M. (1994). *Teacher union bargaining: Practice and policy.* Chicago: Precept Press.

Hersey, P., Blanchard, K. H. & Johnson, D. E. (1996). *The management of organizational behavior.* (7th ed.). Upper Saddle River, NJ: Prentice Hall.

Hoy, W. K. & Miskel, C. G. (1991). *Educational administration: Theory, research, practice.* (4th ed.) NY: McGraw-Hill.

Kahne, J. (1996). *Reframing educational policy: Democracy, community, and the individual.* NY: Teachers College Press.

Lewis, A. (1989). *Restructuring America's schools.* Arlington, VA: AASA Publications.

Robbins, S. P. (1997). *Managing today!* Upper Saddle River, NJ: Prentice Hall.

CHAPTER 14

Community Perspective and Central Office Functions

Every parent sends his or her child to school with the expectation that teachers will provide that child with the skills necessary to be a successful citizen in a changing world. Each parent remembers his or her years in school and expects the same or a better experience for present-day students. School personnel must realize this and factor parental and factor community perspectives and needs into decision making and restructuring.

IT is frequently the case that educational decisions are made within schools without reference to community conditions and needs. The assumption of many educators is that we have the answers and knowledge necessary to provide for children. This assumption is born of external expectations, our own experience of teacher behavior when we were in school, and years of working as teachers in a classroom. Consequently, interference by others is often neither appreciated nor accepted.

What we must realize and remember, however, is that the community has a vested interest in everything educators do. The community has given us its financial support (money) and the care of its children. Our constituents in the community tend to judge educators and education based in large part on the memories of their school experiences and upon the perceptions of others.

Community silence must never be construed to mean approval of all that transpires in schools in general and in classrooms in particular. Sometimes that silence relates to a general inertia within the community or with feelings of powerlessness among the parents of some students, particularly those parents who are not highly educated or who are from the lower socioeconomic status of the society. Virtually every parent or patron will react vocally at some time to situations, whether perceived or real, in which their own children or their schools are negatively impacted by decisions.

In fact, in our American society, governed as it is by the trends of the marketplace, public opinion is formed by schools, nonprint media, and advertisers (Kierstead & Wagner, 1993). The category of nonprint media includes rock stars, movie stars, television, commentators, and so on. In many communities the print and nonprint media carry more credence than does the school. In fact, even in small cities and towns, where the schools seem to carry the most impact relative to community values and cultural mores, television is making greater and greater incursions. Against this backdrop schools must work and decisions must be made relative to the academic achievement, safety, and general education of students.

Public involvement in the educational process has historical roots in the United States. From the town council in New England to the advent of the school board, public involvement has always been a recognized process and an expectation. Even in private and parochial schools, where the relationship between parent or patron and school is contractual, this involvement is expected and generally is apparent.

Only in recent years have some parents, notably those who are of lower socioeconomic status, seemed to feel "put off" by the prospect of going to the school or sharing their opinions concerning the needs of their children. Without speculating on reasons for this perceptual change, suffice it to say that parents must be full partners in the education of their children if expected educational outcomes are to be achieved.

PRODUCTIVE STRUCTURAL CHANGE

For purposes of discussion, structural change should be construed to relate to any variation in district organization, including the reassignment of staff, realignment of responsibilities, addition or deletion of transportation provisions for students, restructuring of grades within schools, or the closing of schools or opening of new school sites. Each of these is visible, tangible, perceivable by patrons and therefore will garner direct and indirect public response.

The intensity of those responses will be in direct proportion to the degree to which a community member's own child is impacted by the change. For example, a change in the opening times of secondary schools generally will not faze the parent of an elementary student, but if that time change causes a time change at the elementary level, there will be any number of patrons with elementary students who will be apt to complain. However, if the contemplated changes can be shared and the bases explained, even if only by means of a letter home, prior to implementation, there will be a higher probability of acceptance by those who are affected.

The optimal scenario, however, is to invite parents and other patrons who represent the various constituencies within the school district to participate in developing the recommendations that will lead to administrator- and board-mandated changes. Participation and the consequent feeling of ownership in the resolution to a problem are crucial in the change process. This in no way implies that the approach central office decision makers must take is purely utilitarian. It is naive to assume that all will be happy with a decision or that even the majority of the patrons and students will be happy with a decision at a given time. However, participative decision making does foster understanding and enhances communication within the district and among all stakeholders.

Additionally, the media is a vehicle that can afford an opportunity to "get the story" out concerning reasons for considering changes in program or services or district procedures. A key component of effective communication with the public is getting individuals "ready" to receive information and to participate in the process of decision making or to provide support for contemplated change.

An understanding of the culture of the community in which the schools are located is crucial to successful implementation of change. Such an understanding will enable school personnel to know what can be changed and what rituals or practices are "sacred" within the community and the schools (Carlson & Awkerman, 1991, p. 54).

Superintendents, boards, principals, and other administrators who disregard this information are creating rather than blunting opposition to proposed changes and may be ensuring that the proposed changes will never be implemented. "The wise administrator accepts and anticipates the entwined complexities (of culture) and proceeds cautiously" (p. 58).

It is important that central office administrators realize that changes must reflect the needs of students and schools. It is also crucial to understand that involving others does not mitigate the responsibility and accountability the central administrator has for appropriate actions in addressing planning and change processes. A key constituency, whenever any change is to be made, is comprised of the school staff and leadership. "To the extent that they (teachers and school administrators) are permitted to fashion the curriculum and the procedures of the school, they will . . . positively influence the social attitudes, ideals and behavior of the coming generation" (Stevens & Wood, 1995, p. 152).

Involvement breeds ownership. No matter what the verbal commitment to change, the actions of principals and teachers will speak volumes with regard to whether or not they are committed to the proposed modifications. That message will be received and believed by parents and students alike.

Communication with all stakeholders and provision of clear information is one way to limit resistance among these individuals. Shared decision making coupled with the expenditure of those personal and objective resources necessary for the facilitation of change will help also to garner support from school-based personnel (Robbins, 1997). It is true that people support changes with which they are comfortable and which they helped to plan and implement. It is also true that for most school district patrons, the first and often only level of contact with the district is at the school site, with the classroom teacher and/or the principal.

Communication is of no value without credibility, however. How is credibility built within an organization? The answer is simple, but the process may not be. Trust, whether within the community or among members of the teaching, administrative, and support staffs within a school district, can be built only over time. Trust building must begin long before the proposal for change is introduced. Only with that trust in the decision-making process can involvement in decision making be substantive and based on open communication.

If plans are made to restructure the district, to open or close a school, or to take any other action that directly affects children, the consideration of the plan should be announced in advance. Public discussion should be encouraged. Clarification and additional information may be offered via the appearance of the superintendent or school administrative staff on talk shows and/or by means of columns written in the local press. Familiarity and comfort with changes before they occur, coupled with the involvement of appropriate parties in decision making, produce "buy in" and support from constituents.

CURRICULAR CHANGES

Curriculum is the legal tender of education. While changes in curriculum may not evoke public response as quickly as other palpable structural changes, nonetheless, patrons and staff alike will fight changes that they believe to be detrimental to the achievement of children or that conflict with their own beliefs relative to what a student must learn in order to be a successful citizen. This is one among many reasons why values education engenders so much debate in some communities. Another reason is that parents sometimes define character or values education as religious in nature and therefore reject the concept of teachers engaging in conveying such information to their children. Again, adequate involvement and communication can do much to allay fears while simultaneously allowing teachers freedom to teach within their spheres of academic competency.

In change efforts, both vision and message will be received with greater credibility and acceptance if the following thoughtful planning and presentation components are in place. Among these components are the following:

- Information conveyed relates to group or community values and beliefs.
- Both sides of the issue are presented in an objective manner.
- Opportunities for questions and discussion are provided.

In the realm of curricular change, questions may arise regarding textbooks and other materials that will be employed as tools for presenting the curriculum. In the present philosophical milieu in the United States, such questions tend to reflect the religious and political views of constituents and may not demonstrate confidence in the ability or interest of the educator to remain objective in the instructional process.

There are certain words and concepts that tend to inflame passions. Among these are "humanism," "values," "outcomes based education," and "critical thinking skills." The difficulty with the appearance of such terminology in the written and taught curriculum, as well as in texts and consumable materials, is that their basic definitions may not be shared by educators and stakeholders in the educational process. In T. H. White's (1959) book *The Once and Future King,* Merlin makes a statement regarding the importance of defining one's terms in order to engage in meaningful conversation. This is precisely the difficulty with curriculum and textbook adoption. Variant definitions of terms may be the root cause of misunderstandings and conflict within a school district.

In an urban school district recently, a children's book was assigned in class. The author of the book had won national recognition for the book. The story, which features a good witch, is interesting, and the graphics are quite good. Several patrons of the district objected strenuously to the presence of the book not only in the classroom but also in the school library. Based on a stated concern about teaching children about evil, the complaint was taken through the district administrative levels and to the school board. Upon review of the book by several disinterested parties within and outside of the district, the book was left on the shelves of the schools but the parents were given the option to allow their children to read something else.

This story is representative of precisely the kind of issues that can arise relative to curriculum content, texts chosen, and the taught curriculum, that is, that which a teacher actually teaches in the classroom. While it is true that there is little possibility of totally avoiding such complaints or confrontations, there is a strong possibility of diffusing potentially time-consuming, divisive curricular debates if the community is involved in decision making through the use of community representation on district and school committees. The credibility brought by having laypeople as part of district processes more than compensates for any accommodations that might need to be made to ensure their active involvement.

BUILDING COMMUNITY CAPACITY

Crucial to the process of obtaining community support and of working within the mores of the community in the education of its children is inculcating capacity. In this context the term *capacity* will be construed to refer to knowledge base and skills. Although it is true that every citizen within a community has some knowledge of education, it is also true that the knowledge is limited by the type of exposure and experiences the individual had as a student in school, as a parent of students attending a school, or via information provided in the media or by word of mouth. Building capacity implies more than involvement, however.

According to Sergiovanni (1990), the steps include:

- creating a feeling of belonging
- building support
- inspiring and bonding through goal focus or purpose
- building a system for automatic improvement

Although educators, particularly teachers and building principals, do recognize the importance of parental and community involvement, since that involvement is sometimes confrontational, they often do not actively pursue parental involvement as a goal. It is therefore the role of central office administrators to encourage, facilitate, and model receptivity to parental assistance in all decisions related to children. These, of course, will relate to curriculum, texts, and general district school organization.

Sometimes, too, parents will ask for the opportunity to express their opinions in regard to personnel matters. Although this is an area of administrative concern, the presence of a parent representative and of a teacher representative on teams that recommend individuals for hiring as principals, for example, may be a valid and valuable idea. It must be made clear that the final decision is not theirs. Nonetheless, the concepts of ownership in the process and participation in planning and decision making can be helpful tools for establishing trust and credibility on the part of school and district personnel.

Trust and credibility will be helpful when controversial or difficult decisions must be made. Individuals who are involved in the school or the district are more likely to ask questions and seek to understand the reasoning behind decisions than are those who have no sense of belonging or involvement. Individuals who are knowledgeable and invested in the district or school are also likely to encourage others to reserve judgment until they understand the ramifications of and reasons for central office and school board actions.

Researchers such as Purkey and Smith (1983) have found that obtaining parent involvement is likely to influence student achievement positively. Parental involvement can lead to greater community involvement as well. The more involved community members are, the greater will be their support not only for changes that are made but also for the millages the district must raise from time to time to support the educational process.

METHODS FOR ENGAGING THE COMMUNITY

It is important to remember that teachers and other district employees are a crucial part of the community. In fact, teachers can be the best or the worst public relations officers for a district. Their credibility is high and their community impact great. Positive attitudes and understandings with regard to district mission, goals, plans, and actions are essential for a teacher or for any other staff member (custodian, cafeteria worker, clerical worker, etc.).

How can the central office garner and ensure such support? How can positive community perspectives be maintained and negative perceptions changed? First, the central office must decide what problems or successes need to be addressed. It can publish newsletters and spread the word through key communicators in schools, parent organizations, and the media. Information can be presented also at community forums such as a Rotary or Kiwanis club, which can be addressed by the superintendent or a board member. Second, agreement should be reached concerning the reasons for success and/or the causes of problems. Finally, develop an action plan that will be effective and inclusive to replicate the success and address the causes of problems.

It is the responsibility of central office personnel to monitor these processes and to ensure that all efforts are directly related to improving instruction and the achievement of the children whom parents send to us and for whom we are responsible as educators and educational leaders. If parents entrust their children to us, they expect our best educational efforts in return.

Regardless of the quality of those efforts as manifested in curriculum and instruction, however, the best insurance of parental and community support is to be found in communication and involvement. Only through these approaches can central office administrators and all other educators ensure a partnership for education by means of developing and considering community perspectives, values, and culture in the educational process. "It is important to realize that matters of equality, fairness, and justice are not simply worked out in the abstract" (Stevens & Wood, 1995, p. 9). Neither is the education of America's youth.

REFERENCES

Carlson, R. V. & Awkerman, G. (eds.). (1991). *Educational planning: Concepts, strategies, and practices.* NY: Longman.

Kierstead, F. D. & Wagner, P. A. (1993). *The ethical, legal, and multicultural foundations of teaching.* Madison, WI: Brown & Benchmark.

Purkey, S. C. & Smith, M. S. (March, 1983). "Effective schools: A review." *The elementary school journal.* 83: 427–452.

Robbins, S. P. (1997). *Managing today!* Saddle River, NJ: Prentice-Hall.

Sergiovanni, T. (1990). *Value-added leadership: How to get extraordinary performance in schools.* San Diego: Harcourt Brace Jovanovich.

Stevens, E., Jr. & Wood, G. H. (1995). *Justice, ideology and education: An introduction to the social foundations of education.* (3rd. ed.) NY: McGraw-Hill.

White, T. H. (1959). *The once and future king.* London: Collin.

CHAPTER 15

Current Issues and Future Trends in Central Office Administration

> While struggling with the ramifications of a decision to empower teachers and stakeholders in the daily education processes that affect children, the district, represented by central office administrators and the school board, is determining its own direction and the direction of K–12 education for the foreseeable future.

FOR more than three decades, Americans have been told that education is at a crossroads and that our educational efforts and our product, the students who graduate from our schools, are substandard when measured against student achievement in other industrialized nations. From the Sputnik crisis (1957), to the National Governors' Association efforts published as *Time for Results* (1987), to national goals, Goals 2000, and the current national effort to educate everyone to at least grade 14, the message has been consistent. That message is that the American educational system does not meet world standards. Whether this allegation is true or false, it must be vigorously addressed.

In the past several decades, educators have responded by calling for more support for educational efforts, spending more money on education, trying new approaches to mathematics and language arts, and blaming society for the woes of its youth. Federal, state, and local governments have responded by demanding reform, testing teachers, testing students, enacting legislation setting curricular standards, and, occasionally, allocating more funds for education. All of this has been done with much discussion in the press and considerable national debate.

MODELS OF SUCCESSFUL CHANGE

In a few situations, however, some educators have quietly dared to experiment with change and have made a difference. Wilson and Daviss (1994) identify some of these efforts and individuals in *Redesigning Education*. One such experiment that has produced major change in student achievement is Reading Recovery, which was developed by Dr. Marie Clay. Other efforts include those made by Principal Rodolfo S. Bernardo in Dayton, Ohio, at the Allen School, and the HIPPY program, created in Israel and brought to the attention of educators in the United States in the 1980s.

Bernardo became principal of a school of low-achieving, lower socioeconomic students whose behavior was problematic. Within five years, the disciplinary sanctions were reduced by more than 95% and student achievement had made significant gains. The composition of the student body did not change; rather, changes were made in the way that these students were taught and in teacher and parental expectations.

In Chicago several years ago, Marva Collins began a school primarily focused on the expectation that all children can learn. She and her students have proven this to be the case. All students can be successful and achieve in their own time and in their own ways. In fact, the recent brain research of Howard Gardner, Eric Goleman, and others supports the experience of Collins's students and teachers. Students who are taught employing instructional methods that reflect their learning styles or frames of intelligence will tend to be more successful, assuming that they are motivated to learn and spend an appropriate amount of time on task.

Of course, parental involvement and high expectations are crucial for learning. The research of Ron Edmonds, Purkey and Smith, Levine, and other educators (Glickman, Gordon & Ross-Gordon, 1995) relative to the components of effective schools identifies these two characteristics (among others). In each of the schools or programs just discussed, high expectations and parental involvement are stressed as well. In the HIPPY program, the Home Instruction Program for Preschool Youth, parental involvement is the key to student learning. Developed in Israel by Dr. A. Lombard, HIPPY is based on training parents to become the teachers of their children. The idea is to train the parents in literacy so that subsequently the parents will train their children and the children of others in preliteracy skills. Reading readiness skills include learning the alphabet, colors, shapes, numerals, and letter sounds. The program trainers provide parents with materials needed to assist in the teaching process, including stories to be read to the children.

In a study published in 1994, Lee and Smith note that there is "compelling evidence that restructuring high schools can indeed make a difference for students." (p. 1) A major component of the restructuring in the high schools studied was community building. Implicit in this concept is the diminishment of the amount of bureaucracy in the school. Additionally, the teachers were encouraged to try innovations, to experiment with instruction, and to collaborate with each other. Complicated rules and procedures were minimized, and teachers were given shared responsibility for decision making. The research study found that in schools where such approaches were used, student achievement increased and that increase was distributed more equitably among all students than in schools with traditional structures (p. 5). Such can be the case in all schools, not only high schools.

APPLICATION TO SCHOOL DISTRICTS

The implications of this research in relation to school districts are many and varied. In the first place, the issue of collaboration is crucial in addressing the needs of teachers and other constituents within school districts. Second, bureaucracy may benefit but often slows the process of education. A common complaint of schoolteachers and administrators is that there is too much bureaucracy and too much paperwork. Consequently, the argument is that it is not worth the effort to try to garner approval for new programs and approaches or to seek a waiver from state curricular regulations and requirements.

Whether or not the complaint is shared by all teachers and administrators and whether or not the complaint is valid are not the major issues. As long as the perception exists that it is not worthwhile to attempt new approaches to enhance student achievement, schools and classrooms will continue to function as they have during the past several decades, that is, in a factory model. Student achievement will doubtless continue to decline or to hold steady at an unacceptable level in the estimation of most Americans.

POSSIBLE SCENARIOS FROM RESTRUCTURING

Restructuring the school district by means of personnel development programs, flattening of the organizational chart, greater involvement of constituencies, encouraging innovation, and replicating successes can do much to improve student achievement. Such changes, coupled with recognition for those who are successful, can enhance motivation of teachers, students, and all who are involved in the education of children.

The issue faced by educators is no longer whether or not all children can learn but rather, given the fact that all children *must* learn, how can that learning be maximized? "Our society simply cannot be sustained as a democracy unless all people are active, contributing, and empowered members of our cultures" (Mellencamp in Mathis et al., 1994, p. 172). Administrators and teachers must be encouraged to learn to be risk takers. They must be able to present knowledge in innovative and multiple approaches to meet the varied abilities of all the students. Efforts must be focused primarily on the students, reflecting their individual learning styles.

Financial efforts and human capital should be focused on the school rather than on district-level personnel. Of course, the implication is not that central office is no longer necessary but that central office must not be an authoritarian power center but should be the facilitator, the support, the vital link in encouraging change. This can be achieved through the use of incentives for successful teachers and the empowerment of school staffs, allowing them to vary the structure of the day and school year in order to maximize instructional time. Teachers, those closest to the students, must be included in a meaningful way in decision making relative to curriculum, disciplinary policy, and instructional practices.

Parents must be engaged as full partners in the process. To achieve this end, some schools have begun to operate on a contractual basis with parents. Taking an example from private and parochial institutions, some public schools are requiring parents to sign a contract that guarantees that they will be in attendance for at least one parent meeting and that they will participate in the child's class at least one full day during the year. Furthermore, these parents are asked to work each evening with the student on homework and to discuss events and current lessons of the school day. The Tempe, Arizona, school district is one of the districts using contractual agreements with parents.

For its part, the school provides parents with a copy of the curriculum guide, which includes the skills to be acquired and concepts to be mastered by that student in his or her grade and class during each quarter of the school year. This is both helpful to the parents and a commitment on the part of the school and its teachers to accountability for student learning and mastery of subject matter and skills.

Superintendents and school boards must be visible and vocal leaders in this change. They should ensure that parents are informed of the concept and skills to be mastered by their children at each grade level. Provision should be made for parent centers where parents, even those with low levels of literacy, can learn how to assist their students with their studies. At such centers, parents may also enhance their own skills.

Other schools have restructured their institutions by opening the high schools to adult (G.E.D.) students. The result has been that students and their parents or neighbors learn together. (The presence of adults in the school has an additional benefit, namely that of helping to improve classroom discipline.) School boards and central office administrators who are reluctant to take this approach or who find that space does not allow restructuring may choose to open schools at night and pay teachers an additional stipend to provide adult education. Education for students who may not be able to attend during the regular day for a variety of reasons, including but not limited to teen parenthood, may complete their high school education at night also.

Still other schools have proposed and districts have supported the creation of accelerated programs for students who are likely dropouts. Such programs allow self-paced learning and do not hold students in place simply because attendance based on the number of days in the semester or year has not been fulfilled. [The only requirement is that adequate seat time be in place for the student to receive the appropriate Carnegie credit(s).]

Some schools and districts have reached out into their communities to form partnerships with higher education. Facilitated but not managed by central office administrators, such partnerships enable teachers in the school district and higher educators to learn from each other to the benefit of students. A few such initiatives have been:

- social casework interns assisting with interventions at the junior high school, thereby benefiting both the students at the junior high and the students in the professional school
- high school teachers teaching courses that are accorded credit both at the high school and the area university. Although this is not an Advanced Placement program, it provides a monetary savings for the parents of those students, recognition for the expertise of the high school teacher, and advancement for the student should he or she wish to attend a college.
- school site councils elected at each school to act not only as a representative of parents/patrons but also to provide support for and advice to the principal and area assistant superintendent, if such exists
- development of distance education and technology-based education programs that maximize dollars and learning
- alternative settings for education coupled with flexible scheduling, that is, the premise under which field trips contribute

to the educational process. Why must it be limited to field trips alone?

- schools within schools, such as the model used in some schools in the Bronx in the New York City system

REQUIREMENTS FOR RESTRUCTURING

Provision must be made to educate teachers and principals in decision-making skills such as nominal group, fishbowl, and brainstorming techniques. Teachers, administrators, and indeed all staff members, including the central office staff and school board, should receive training in addressing the needs of diverse populations of students.

Beyond that, each administrator, teacher, and board member should be comfortable with proposed changes or they will not be well implemented. In fact, although behaviors may change by mandate, attitudes and beliefs do not change in that way. Attitudes and beliefs change only over time and only if based in trust and understanding of what is to be changed and how it will benefit students, patrons, and, above all, the individual who is asked to adopt the desired new behaviors or practices.

Professional development training must be ongoing, not relegated to one session or a single in-service time. In fact, professional development must be grounded in adult learning theory. Adult learning theory posits that adults must be approached and taught in a different manner from student learners in K–12. Most teachers and administrators have not been schooled in addressing adult needs. Adults are more judgmental than K–12 students, and they tend to need to reflect on ideas prior to responding to them. Adult learners require active engagement in the learning. (Of course, many elementary and secondary students need the same kind of involvement, but problematically, some teachers are not capable of creating such student involvement in learning activities and prefer frontal lecture as a method of instruction.)

Additional training must prepare the school community and patrons to be receptive to any additional activities if they are to benefit from them. They must share the vision and perceive the needs of those who are to benefit from the end product that they are restructuring to produce. Teachers must also realize that extra training is of paramount importance in their preparation for the implementation of educational change.

Unless and until this is true, teachers, administrators, and community members will not be receptive to such activities. The stakeholders must know that the restructuring about which they are to be trained is compatiblc with the purpose of the organization and will benefit them and the students. Finally, they need to know that issues regarding physical, financial, and human resources have been considered and that the restructuring will be efficient and effective in all of these areas (Maxwell, 1993).

Another requirement for restructuring is that the board and superintendent should be willing to move central office staff out of their offices, both literally and figuratively. As is the case with teachers, good educators who are administrators must do their paperwork after hours and at home. The real focus of all educators must be student learning. Assignment of personnel, particularly central office personnel, in new ways that do not parallel business organizational structure but which place support staff in schools on a regular basis is an important component of restructuring (see Chapter 13).

PROBABLE SCENARIOS IF CHANGE DOES NOT OCCUR

School boards and the superintendency as we have known them in the past may well begin to disappear from the educational scene if student achievement and school organizational issues are not addressed and remedied. Currently, President Bill Clinton has called for national testing. During recent past administrations, the U.S. Congress has passed legislation mandating national educational goals and the Office of Educational Research in the U.S. Department of Education has produced several sets of national curricular frameworks for consideration by states and school districts. Never before has the involvement of the federal government been so extensive as it relates to education.

In cities such as Washington, D.C., and Chicago, the school board has ceased to exist in the mode that has become a tradition in this country. In the District of Columbia, it has simply been abolished. In Chicago, the policy-making board has been replaced by a board of businesspeople who are responsible for fiscal and organizational decisions in the district and who are operating the district as if it were a business. While there are major business components to the daily operations of school districts, as has previously been discussed in this text, nonetheless, the primary focus of school districts is or should be educational.

Although two examples do not necessarily represent a trend, there is always the possibility that they are the seeds of major and substantial change in educational governance. If the "system" of school board and superintendent is to remain operative in our public schools, it would seem that the time has arrived for significant restructuring to take place in order to enhance the education of students, improve achievement, and reflect the changing demands and needs of the marketplace. Failure to do so may result in significant changes in the control and direction of American education.

The home schooling, voucher, and charter school movements are but the tip of the iceberg. They cannot be ignored nor can educators and those who prepare and hire educators and administrators fail to recognize that changes in educational practice are essential. The educational models of the 1950s and 1960s simply do not meet the needs of the clientele schools serve today. Legislators, parents, and students have demonstrated over the past few years that indeed schooling is subject to the same parameters as general private sector commerce and services. "Change will come. Will [central office administrators and school boards] . . . lead or be pulled into a new model of education without the change to be part of the process?" (Sewall, 1997, p. 41). As noted by Wilson and Daviss (1994), "A future that holds change as the only constant leaves us no choice" (p. 229).

REFERENCES

Gardner, H. (1983). *Frames of mind: The theory of multiple intelligences.* NY: Basic Books.

Glickman, C. D., Gordon, S. P. & Ross-Gordon, J. M. (1995). *Supervision of instruction: A developmental approach.* Boston: Allyn & Bacon.

Goleman, D. (1995). *Emotional intelligence: Why it can matter more than IQ.* NY: Bantam Books.

Lee, V. E. & Smith, J. B. (1994). "High school restructuring and student achievement: A new study finds strong links." *Issues in restructuring schools.* Madison, WI: Center on Organization and Restructuring of Schools.

Mathis, W. J. et al. (1994). *Field guide to educational renewal: Vermont restructuring collaborative.* Brandon, VT: Holistic Education Press, Inc.

Maxwell, J. C. (1993). *Developing the leader within you.* Nashville, TN: Thomas Nelson Publishers.

Sewall, A. M. (1997). "Accountability and teacher education." *National Forum: The Phi Kappa Phi Journal.* 77(1): 38–41.

Wagner, T. (February, 1997). "The new village commons–Improving schools together." *Educational Leadership.* 25–28.

Wilson, K. G. & Daviss, B. (1994). *Redesigning education.* NewYork: Henry Holt and Company, Inc.

Academic achievement, 16, 148-156
   and parents, 149-150
   of students, 149-150
Accountability, 12, 15, 47, 51
   and funding, 47
   and student learning, 75, 78
Action research, 48, 49, 64, 65, 93
Affirmative action, 133
Americans with Disabilities Act
   (A.D.A.), 27, 31, 35, 37, 79-81
Alignment (curricular), 55
Articulation (curricular), 55
Assessment (*see also* evaluation), 69,
   93-96, 100
Assistant superintendent, 12-15, 130
Associate superintendent, 15, 131
"At risk", 86, 87
Attendance, 98
Authority, 4, 15, 26, 132, 133

Block grants, 40, 41, 47
Budget, 18, 26, 100, 103-105
Business Functions, 97-106

Capital outlay, 98
Categorical grants, 47
Central Office, 4, 6, 7, 9, 23, 26, 46, 61,
   85, 92
Chapter I (*see also* Title 1), 32, 34
Charter School, xii, 6, 31
Child Nutrition Act, 38
Collaboration (*see* teaming), 21, 63, 64
Commissioner of Education (see state

school officer), 43
Communication, 11, 12, 20, 66, 109, 124,
   140
Chapter II, 33
Communicator, 11, 19
Community, 10, 12, 66, 136-144
   community capacity, 134-137
   learning community, 65, 68, 141-142
Compensatory education, 47, 82, 83
Constitutional issues, 1, 119-122
Contract, 9, 19, 20, 71
Construction, 3, 102
Culture, 18
Curriculum, 3, 4, 12, 15, 51-72, 97, 104,
   140
   and curriculum guides, 53, 57, 148
   and curriculum supervisors, 54, 58, 59
   and teachers, 53, 57
   and texts, 18, 55, 148

Data gathering, 99, 100, 135, 136
Debt management, 3
Debt service, 98
Decentralization, 104-105
Deputy superintendent, 15
Desegregation, 3, 123, 124, 133, 134
Direct costs, 98
Discipline, 51, 62, 86-87, 97, 118-120
Driving forces, 91-92
Due process, 71, 120

Eighth Amendment, 119, 120
Emergencies, 14

Encumbrances, 98
Enrollment, 98
ESEA, xii, 27, 31
Evaluation, 3, 27, 71, 93, 96, 100
    formative, 27, 94
    summative, 27, 94
Expulsion, 4

Facilities, 102, 103
Facilitator, 18-21, 46, 97
Finances, 6, 12, 97-105, 123, 124
First Amendment, 122-123
Fixed costs, 98, 103
Food services, 39
Full Time Equivalent (FTE), 54
Fourteenth Amendment, 84, 119-120
Fourth Amendment, 120-121
Funding, 18
    federal funding, 2, 32, 33, 38, 41, 123
    state funding, 2, 43-45, 47, 98, 99
Federal Program, 31

Gifted education, 81-82
Goals, 25, 28, 69, 90
    national goals, 25, 28
Governance, 2, 4, 44, 99

Health issues, 85-86, 134
HIPPY (home instruction program for
    preschool youth), 146, 147
Homeless students, 84, 85
Home school, xii, 6

Inclusion, 36-37, 78, 79
Indirect costs, 98
Individuals with Disabilities
    Education Act (I.D.E.A.)/ P.L., xii,
    27, 31, 35, 76
Innovation, 13
In-service (staff development), 19, 59
Instruction, 15, 16, 67-69, 97
Instructional leadership, 16, 51-73, 100

Judicial role (of school board), 4, 24-29

Leader, 16-19
Leadership, 18, 21, 107
Leadership style, 17-18
Legal issues, 31, 33, 70, 72, 117-125

Legal status, 3, 125

Mainstreaming, 77-78
Maintenance, 100, 105
Manager, 12
Media (press), 19, 107-115
Membership (student), 3, 98
Migrant students, 84, 85
Millage, 18, 98-99, 112-114
Mission, 16, 27, 89-90
Monitoring, 99

National Goals, 5, 33, 45, 145
National Governors' Association, 5, 6,
    45, 53
Noncertified, 3
National School Board Association, 24

Objectives, 28, 55, 90, 91
Organizational charts, 13, 14, 15
Organizational patterns, 13-15

Per pupil expenditures, 40, 98
Personnel, 12, 44, 62-64, 65-66, 105
Planning, 3, 25, 41, 89-92, 136
Planning levels (mega, macro, micro), 25,
    90-96
Policy, 1, 12, 23-29, 38, 108-109
    and law, 27-28
    and review, 27-28
    and site-based management, 26-27
    and students, 24
Politician, 11, 20
Politics, 10, 11, 20
Power, 4, 132
Precedent, 75
Principl, 12-15, 17-18, 62, 117
Professional development, 19, 59,
    66-67
Property tax, 5
Public relations, 19, 24, 107-115
Purchasing, 3, 105

Reading recovery, 146
Reform, 5, 6, 28-29, 40, 75
Resources, 4, 103-105, 124
Restraining forces, 91-92
Restructuring, 10, 40, 46, 51, 66, 68,
    127-135, 138-139, 147-150

Rights, 120
  civil, 117-124
  due process, 120
  privacy, 120-121
  and responsibilities, 123-124
  student, 122-123

SBM, 5, 9, 13, 16, 26, 34, 63, 104, 118, 121
School Board, 2-4, 9, 10-22
  and budget, 98, 104
  and curriculum, 57, 148
  and policy, 9, 23-24
  responsibilities, 27, 129
  roles, 4, 108, 124, 148
  and staff, 9, 62-63
  powers, 4
  and superintendent, 11, 16
  training, 16-17
School Lunch Act, 31, 38
Section 504, xii, 31, 35, 37-38, 79-81
Site-based management, 9, 13, 16, 26, 34,
    40, 63, 104
Special education (see IDEA), 35-37,
    75-81
Standards, 43
  national, 33, 45, 56
  re: space, 103
  state, 53, 56, 103
State school officer, 43
  Association of State School
  Officers, 45
Strategies, 90-91
Superintendent, 3-5, 9-22
  as communicator, 12, 63
  and finances, 124
  and issues, 125
  as leader, facilitator,

  manager, 9-21
  and personnel, 62-64
  as politician, 11, 20
  and style, 17
  and poetry, 4, 9
  roles, 9-22
  search, 20-21
  and schoolboard 9, 19-20
  and vision, 63

Teaming (team building), 20, 63, 64, 82
Technology, 16, 99-101
Tenth amendment, 1
Tenure, 10, 21, 25
Termination, 3, 4, 10, 20, 62
Testing, 43, 56
Title 1, 16, 31, 33, 34
Transactional leadership, 83, 107
Transformational leadership, 83, 107
Transportation, 3, 12, 99

Unrestricted funds, 98
U.S. Constitution, 1
U.S. Department of Education, 5, 45-46

Variable costs, 98
Vision, 4, 25, 27, 89-90, 107, 136
Vocational education, 83-84

Warehousing, 12, 105
  Welfare (of students), 31-41, 75-87

Title II, 32
Title VI, 133
Title VII, 31
Title IX, 31, 133